HOW TO ARGUE WITH ANYONE

EXPAND THE BOUNDARIES OF YOUR THINKING
THROUGH RESOLVING CONFLICTS BASED ON
REASON AND EMPATHY

THINKNETIC

GET 3 FREE BONUSES!

Free Bonus #1
Our Bestseller *Critical Thinking In A Nutshell*

Did You Know That 93% Of CEOs Agree That This Skill Is More Important Than Your College Degree?

Here's just a fraction of what you'll discover inside:

- How to shortcut the famous Malcom Gladwell "10,000 Hours Rule" to become an expert critical thinker, fast
- What a WW2 pilot and the people of Romania can teach you about critical thinking - this is the KEY to not making huge mistakes
- Actionable, easy exercises to drill home every point covered in the novel. You won't "read and forget" this book

"This book is a good primer for the beginner and a good refresh for the expert who wants to bring more critical thinking into their problem-solving. Easy to read and understand, buy this book."

(Kevin on April 19, 2021)

"This book is unlike any other on Critical Thinking. The author puts an entirely new twist in critical thinking. Very easy to understand. Give it a read and see for yourself."

(Knowledge Seeker on April 16, 2021)

"The explanations are straight forward, sensible and usable with some interesting ideas about how this can be taught or learned."

(Dave Crisp on April 14, 2021)

Free Bonus #2
Thinking Cheat Sheet *Break Your Thinking Patterns*

Free Bonus #3
Thinking Guide *Flex Your Wisdom Muscle*

<u>A glimpse into what you'll discover inside:</u>

- If your thinking is flawed and what it takes to fix it (the solutions are included)
- Tried and true hacks to elevate your rationality and change your life for the better
- Enlightening principles to guide your thoughts and actions (gathered from the wisest men of all time)

Go to thinknetic.net to download for free!

(Or simply scan the code with your camera)

SCAN ME

INTRODUCTION

How do you know if you've had a good argument? Is it when the other person changes their opinion? Is it when you walk away even more confident in your own beliefs than before?

The reality of a good argument is, for better or worse, much more complicated.

How many times have you walked away from an argument feeling pleased that the other person agreed with you – only to have the *exact same* argument bubble up again a few days later? How often have you apologized or said you were wrong just to end an argument – even if you didn't believe it? How many times have you struggled to get your point across because the other person just seemed to be better at arguing? And how many times have you wanted to bang your head against the wall because the person you were trying to argue with was being so stubborn and unbelievable?

Arguing is important. It can even be fun. But arguing can also be one of the most frustrating things that we do, especially when the other person seems to be just wrong about something but refuses to admit it. Worse, arguing can create grudges and tension that lasts for days or weeks.

Does this mean that we're all doomed to argue endlessly with the people we care about, creating more and more bad feelings? No. There is a better way – a way to argue more effectively while bringing you closer to the people you disagree with, instead of creating bad feelings. That's what this book is about.

Over the course of this book, we'll go through the building blocks of a better argument. Starting with little tricks to improve your logic and expanding to how to deal with irrational conversation partners, we'll look at each aspect of having a better argument. By the end of the book, you'll not only be able to present your opinions more confidently, but you'll also be able to ask better questions and understand the points of value in even the most confusing argument.

The best part is that the strategies in this book work for any argument. You can use the same tactics when arguing with your spouse, friends, coworkers, and even your children. And these strategies work for everyone, whether you enjoy arguing or avoid it like the plague.

I should know – I used to struggle with arguing. My spouse and I didn't argue often, but when we did, it was memorably terrible. We would argue for hours, sometimes not even reaching a resolution after all that time. Then, days or weeks later, the argument would suddenly come back. Arguments with my friends and coworkers were much less tense – because they didn't happen. I preferred nodding along to even the most ridiculous claims instead of arguing, which left me feeling frustrated and unheard.

I made it my mission to learn to argue better. Drawing on my background in psychology and politics, I researched extensively what makes a good argument and how to argue better. Eventually, that research became this book. I know that every strategy works because I've tried it myself.

And it does work. My spouse and I still argue, which I won't claim always goes perfectly. Still, we reach a positive solution every time and agree that we feel closer and more connected after arguing than we did before. Even better, the argument doesn't come back later. Using the same strategies, I can disagree with my friends and coworkers respectfully and constructively instead of avoiding conflict and feeling unheard.

This book will give you a roadmap about how to argue better. It will give you helpful strategies for everything from knowing when to start an argument to using better body language. It won't, however, make you an expert in arguing overnight. That will take practice. You'll need to decide that this is the time to become a better arguer and you'll need to keep working at it, even when things are difficult and arguments go poorly. But, with the strategies in this book, you'll be able to improve your arguments, bit by bit, until you're having exactly the kinds of arguments you want. These solutions are straightforward, give good results, and, best of all, you can start applying them today.

Are you ready to argue better? Are you ready to see the bigger picture of why arguing matters? Are you ready to walk away from arguments feeling positive instead of regretful? Then let's get started.

Davan O'Donnell

1

BACK TO THE BASICS

Have you ever watched a courtroom drama?

The interactions between the lawyers in these dramas are fascinating. They use logic, facts, emotion, and procedure to outline a compelling case that can even, for a moment, make you reconsider whether the defendant is guilty or not. Scenes like "You can't handle the truth!" from *A Few Good Men* stick with us for a long time after we switch off the screen. Both in life and on television, courtrooms are hotbeds for some of the most well-developed, interesting arguments out there. Plus, they always end with a resolution through a verdict.

Of course, these dramatized arguments are very different from those that you or I might have on a day-to-day basis. Real-life arguments are rarely as polished or as convincing. Why do arguments differ so much between different people at different times? What role do arguments play in our daily lives? And why is it important to argue and to argue well?

What Is An Argument?

We've all been there. One moment, you are having a normal conversation. You're chatting easily with your friend, co-worker, or family member. The next moment, things get heated, and opinions start flying – suddenly, it's an argument.

Although arguments are as familiar to most of us as coffee or toast, many people have the wrong idea of what an argument is. Often, people think that an argument is more or less the same as a fight. If people are disagreeing, it's always an argument. Right?

In fact, it's a little more complicated than that. A fight is any disagreement (or heated discussion or brawl). If you are fighting, you and the person you're disagreeing with might just be throwing assertions at each other, such as "You have no idea what you're talking about!" or "You're doing this wrong." Fights are generally about the airing of opinions, while arguments are generally more productive.

Arguments are more nuanced and, when done right, much more productive. Arguments are a societal process of using facts and logic to challenge incorrect opinions. [1] In an argument, you make statements (also called arguments) that support your opinion, with the goal of finding the truth about the topic you are discussing. Instead of just stating what you believe, you are working together with your conversational partner to find a shared, factual understanding.

In an argument, for instance, you might say, "I understand why you believe that you do more chores around the house. But personally, I believe that we do a fairly equal amount because I always clean the bathroom and the kitchen while you always clean the bedroom and the living room." You may go into an argument with the goal of changing someone's opinion, but a good argument can also lead you to change your own opinions. Arguments don't necessarily involve yelling or annoyance. They can also be friendly, calm, positive discussions.

A good argument draws on two things: data and logical arguments to structure that data. [2] Data refers to the facts and evidence on which you base your argument. In later chapters, we'll have a closer look at how to gather good data and make sure that it's accurate and relevant.

We'll start here with logic in arguments. There are multiple types of logical structures that you can use to structure your arguments – we'll have a brief look at a few of them here.

Types Of Arguments

The three basic types of logical arguments are deductive, inductive, and abductive. Deductive arguments start with a main statement or hypothesis, which is then applied to specific situations. [3] Whether or not your argument makes sense comes down to how accurate your main statement is. For instance, your main statement could be that candies are all delicious. Then, if you find a new piece of candy that you've never eaten before, you'll know before you taste it that it must be delicious.

For a more applicable example, say you're disagreeing with the people you live with about whose turn it is to buy milk. You might make a deductive argument as follows: "We alternate whose turn it is to buy milk. So, since it was my turn last week and I brought home a carton, that means it must be your turn this time."

You can also use an inductive argument. Inductive arguments start with observations or statistics which are used to draw a conclusion. [4] They can be very accurate if you have enough data, or very flawed if your argument is based on limited data. For instance, you might reach into a bag of candies and pull out red candies three times in a row. From that, you might deduce that all the candies in the bag are red. This could be true: maybe all the candies are red. But it could also be that there were only three red candies in the bag and all the rest are other colors.

Going back to the milk discussion, you might choose an inductive instead of a deductive argument. You could say, "You forgot to buy milk two weeks ago and last month when it was your turn. So, if someone forgot to buy milk this time, it must have been you."

There are also abductive arguments. In abductive reasoning, you make an educated guess of the most likely explanation for something based on the data you have available. [5]This kind of argument is the least logical, because it's based on some guesswork, but can still be accurate. A jury trying to find out if a suspect is guilty of robbery usually uses abductive reasoning to examine whatever evidence they have to reach a conclusion.

In the milk situation, you might use abductive reasoning to say, "there's no milk in the fridge, so you must have forgotten to buy it."

Beyond the three basic types of arguments, there are a few more possibilities for argument structures that are more nuanced. Stephen Toulmin developed the Toulmin style of arguments back in the 1950s. His arguments have several factors: claim, grounds, warrant, qualifier, rebuttal, and backing. [6] This may sound complex, but it actually draws heavily on both inductive and deductive arguments.

In Toulmin's arguments, you begin with a claim, similar to your main statement in deductive reasoning. You then find the grounds, evidence, or data to support your claim. Next, you link them with a warrant. For instance, you might claim that China has the best divers in the world. To back this up, you might note the grounds that the Chinese team has won the highest percentage of Olympic medals. [7] Then you'll connect them with a warrant, which may be that winning Olympic medals points to skill in any sport. Qualifiers, rebuttals, and backing are additional ways to support your argument by making it specific, responding to critiques, and supplying additional evidence.

A rebuttal argument may be viewed as a type of argument all on its own, in which your argument is focused on disproving and contradicting your conversation partner. [8]

In the case of the milk debate, you might say: "You are the one who forgot to buy the milk. There's no milk in the fridge, and I bought the milk last time. So, this time it's your turn."

Classical Western arguments, on the other hand, draw on logic as well as other factors. In a Classical argument, you draw on four strategies to convince your conversation partner to agree with you. These four strategies are:

1. Ethos - your credibility or character. When you draw on Ethos, you are offering your credentials and experience that make you a trustworthy source of information on a topic in question.

2. Logos - the logical, factual structure of your argument. When drawing on Logos, you put together statements and facts in a compelling way.

3. Pathos - the emotional side of your argument. When you draw on Pathos, you reach out to your conversation partner's feelings.

4. Kairos - the temporal side of your argument. You might say that there is limited time to change an opinion or that now is exactly the right time to do so. [9]

When it comes to milk, you might say, "I always keep good track of our shopping list and the milk-buying schedule (Ethos). Since it was my turn last time, this time it is your turn (Logos). We really need milk if we want to have cereal tomorrow, and the store will close in just half an hour (Kairos and Pathos). Will you go buy some?"

Not all arguments are about winning, though. The Rogerian argument offers a different viewpoint on arguing. In a Rogerian argument, your goal is to reach a common ground between you and the person you are arguing with that is mutually acceptable. [10] This happens in three steps:

1. Making your conversation partner feel understood,

2. Outlining the points in which you think your conversation partner is correct,

3. Show that you and your conversation partner have similar values, such as reaching a mutually acceptable solution. [11]

Rogerian arguments have a lot of benefits. They are useful for arguments with friends, family, and coworkers in which reaching a peaceful and positive conclusion is the most important goal. However, there are drawbacks, too. If the argument centers around science and facts, for instance, it may not be possible to reach a compromise that is also truthful. And, if your conversation partner is only interested in winning, you are unlikely to resolve the argument peacefully anyway

In the milk situation, you might say, "I know that you were really busy today and that you didn't have time to go to the store. I also agree that we are both responsible for making sure we have groceries. How about we go to the store together?"

Similar to Rogerian arguments is the proposal argument. In a proposal argument, your goal is to outline a solution to a problem and, using evidence, convince your conversation partner that you have the best solution.[12] If you are using a proposal argument, you are focused on resolving the issue peacefully, just like in a Rogerian argument.

Meanwhile, the opposite of a proposal argument is a causal argument, in which you focus on finding the cause of a certain problem. [13] This argument is often too focused on placing blame, so it's less likely to lead to a productive conclusion.

With the huge variety of possible arguments out there, how can you decide which is best or most effective? The answer is that it depends hugely on your context and goals. If you get into a debate with your spouse about where you should go on vacation using an inductive argument about how miserable you've been in the past when they chose the destination, you probably aren't going to get good results. On the other hand, if you use a Rogerian argument to pick your next vacation along with your spouse, you might be happier with what happens next.

In our everyday arguments, we usually use a mix of different styles depending on the circumstances, the goal of the conversation, and how the argument unfolds. Which argument works best, and how each type of argument plays out in real life, is something that we'll continue to explore throughout the rest of this book.

Right, Wrong, Or Just Plain Weird

You might go into an argument with the most logical, factual, multi-pronged argument possible – and find that your conversation partner has no idea what they're talking about or is just making things up. In the milk argument, for instance, your conversation partner might say, "I don't even drink milk!" when you see them have a large latte every morning. How can you tell if they are making a fact-based argument or not?

The first and most important thing is to determine the basis of your conversation partner's arguments. Are they drawing on credible sources? If you aren't sure, ask questions about where and when your conversation partner heard the facts that they are stating. If their argument has a factual basis, it's more likely to be valid – although there are still more factors to consider.

Next, think about the logic behind their argument. It's possible to take factual sources and stretch or bend them until they are no longer valid. Perhaps your conversation partner is taking a quote out of context or trying to apply inductive reasoning based on only a single experience. We'll discuss logic and how it can go wrong more deeply in Chapter Three.

When examining the validity of your conversation partner's argument, make sure you think about the validity of your own argument, too. Without meaning to, we can make the same kinds of logical or factual errors as anyone else. Thinking carefully about your opinions and reading books like this are good ways to prevent that.

Why Arguments Start

Another person's illogical or counterfactual statement is one reason that arguments tend to start, although it isn't the only one. There are three main reasons why arguments usually start:

1. The other person has incorrect data or logic;

2. You have incorrect data or logic;

3. You both have different but valid opinions about a complex or emotional topic.

In the first two cases, the argument will likely be resolved by one or the other of you 'winning.' Maybe someone says that the flashing red light on the printer means that it's out of paper because the light flashed once before and stopped when they added more paper. However, you know this isn't true. You show the other person the part of the printer manual where it says that the flashing red light means a paper jam. When the other person added more paper, they also cleared out the old paper, resolving the jam. Unless the other person is in a bad mood or has some very strong opinions about printers, they'll probably change their opinion to agree with you now that they have all the facts. They were wrong about the meaning of the flashing light, while you were right.

Most arguments, however, are more complicated. They start for the third reason on the list: different but valid opinions about a complex or emotional topic. Perhaps you mention to a friend that you try to eat meat at least once a day for protein. They might respond that they are a vegetarian and get their protein from other sources. You can argue about this topic by showing articles and citing experiences that support your point. Neither of you is technically wrong, but there's a low chance of the argument ending with anyone changing their opinion. The third type of argument is the one that we tend to encounter more in daily life. It's also the kind of argument that you can make better with strategies – like the ones we discuss in this book.

Whether or not you like arguing, arguments are an important part of life. From deciding who forgot to buy the milk to choosing a political viewpoint, arguments play a huge role in our choices and relationships. Without arguments, your opinion, and the opinions of those around you, right or wrong, would stay the same. Making and having better arguments means change, growth, and new understanding for everyone involved.

Action Steps

It's time to look more closely at the arguments in your own life. Over the next week or so, keep a log of your arguments. Note who you argued with, how it started, and how the argument was resolved. If possible, keep track of the kinds of logical arguments that you and your conversational partner used (though it's more likely to be a mix of styles than one strict type).

Keep in mind that arguments aren't the same as fights. A debate with a cashier over the sale price of a bar of chocolate should go on your argument list, but a heated discussion with your child about their bedtime might not.

At the end of the week, reflect on the types of arguments that you have and who you tend to argue with. Do you usually argue with coworkers, family, friends, or others? Do some arguments seem to go better than others? If so, do you have any guesses about why that might be? Hold on to your list of arguments as you continue reading this book.

Whether you are a courtroom lawyer or not, arguments play a big role in your life – and always have. Throughout history, humans have had a shifting understanding of what it means to argue and what the most effective strategies are. Throughout, though, arguments have remained an important part of society. In the next chapter, we'll look at that shifting understanding and how it has shaped today's arguments. We'll also assemble time-tested strategies for better arguments, whether in Roman times or modern society.

Chapter Summary

- Arguments are not the same as fights – arguments are focused on logic, facts, and coming to a shared point of view, while fights are often just statements of disagreeing opinions. When you are logically debating an issue with the hope of a good solution, you're having an argument.
- There are multiple argument structures, including deductive, inductive, abductive, Toulmin, Classic Western, and Rogerian. Many real-life arguments draw on a mix of these.
- For an argument to be valid, it must have both correct data and correct logic.
- Arguments usually start because of either incorrect data or logic or because of different but equally valid opinions about a topic.

2

WHY ANCIENT ARGUMENTS MATTER TO YOU

Have you ever been in the middle of an argument when the other person brought up something that happened ages ago? "That's ancient history!" you might have replied. You were probably indignant that they even brought up that old story. Ancient history has no place in everyday arguments, right?

In fact, ancient history plays a key role in every argument. That's because each argument draws on a long tradition of debate across time and place. (Although that's no excuse to bring up old problems in your arguments!) It might not seem like it, but today's arguments use ideas developed hundreds of years ago. And some of the same strategies people used to win arguments hundreds of years ago work just as well today.

A Brief History Of Arguments

Arguments have been a part of history for almost as long as there have been people. The earliest humans developed arguing out of necessity for collaboration and shared understanding of what couldn't be seen. [1] This is easy to imagine: two of the earliest humans might have needed to decide where they could forage for food. One of them might have mentioned previously seeing apples growing on a tree near the river. The other might argue that this is spring, when apples don't grow. Together, they might then decide to try looking for cherries instead.

Over time, arguments have naturally become more complicated than decisions about where to find food or how to avoid predators. Many ancient societies had rich traditions of arguing and debating about a variety of topics. In Ancient Greece, for example, ordinary citizens could participate in the democratic process by voicing reasoned arguments to the democratic assembly. [2] These arguments tended to be long, logical speeches that focused on morals and politics. [3] Ancient Greece was one of the first places where the general population could have a voice, on a large scale, through a good argument.

Meanwhile, ancient India had a culture of arguments, too. These debates were generally between sages and were supported by the rulers of the time, with normal people playing little role. [4] The topics under debate included religion, medicine, and knowledge, with questions such as sources of knowledge and the potential for an afterlife. [5] Ancient Indians also developed an idea of logical fallacies (flaws in the logical process, which we'll discuss in <u>Chapter Three</u>). [6]

The Ancient Chinese valued good arguments as well. These arguments focused on the correct names for different objects and concepts. [7] Just like in Ancient Greece, ancient Chinese arguers were interested in convincing large groups of people of their opinion. [8] The main difference is that in China, these were followers, whereas, in Greece, they were fellow citizens. Chinese arguers were specially trained throughout their lives and were listened to and respected by many people. Greek arguers were not necessarily trained – they could be anyone who happened to have an opinion on the topic of the day.

In all these ancient civilizations, debate evolved independently. The ancient Indians weren't inspired to begin debating by the ancient Chinese, or the other way around. The separate evolution of arguments shows how necessary arguments are in human society – they're as much a part of our society as buildings or food, no matter where we come from. It also shows how much the style and topic of arguments depend on time and place. To look at this a little more closely, let's examine some influential moments in the history of arguments, and the people who inspired them.

Throughout the centuries, a few people have significantly influenced the development of arguments. Drawing from their societies and existing knowledge, each of these people caused arguments to evolve. More importantly for us today, the strategies they used have withstood the test of time and continue to be just as effective today as they were tens or hundreds of years ago. Let's get to know the secrets of some of the greatest arguers of all time.

Sun Tzu

To this day, Sun Tzu is one of the most influential arguers of all time. His book, The Art of War, continues to be read by military commanders and businesspeople to this day, and his wisdom is equally applicable to any argument. There is some debate about whether Sun Tzu really existed, but the existence of The Art of War and its teachings are inarguable.

Sun Tzu argued that war (which we can expand to arguments) is a necessary evil. "If you know the enemy and know yourself, you need not fear the result of a hundred battles," the *Art of War* reads. [9] This may not seem revolutionary, but it was. For many years, people thought that arguments (and wars) could be won by sheer force: good facts and good logic. But Sun Tzu understood that this was not the case. Without knowing the person who you are arguing with, and making the right argument to convince them specifically, you'll never win.

The Greek Trio: Socrates, Plato, And Aristotle

Let's jump halfway around the world to Ancient Greece. There, a student-teacher team revolutionized the way that debates took place throughout the whole of Greek society. That team was Plato and Socrates. Plato drew on Socrates' teachings to propose a new style of debate. Instead of long speeches, he preferred quick discussions full of back and forth. This style of argument is known as a dialectic encounter and has a lot in common with today's informal arguments.

The third in the trio, Aristotle, took dialectic encounters one step further. He emphasized the importation of refutation. [10] Instead of just making logical statements, a debater needs to be able to prove the other person's arguments wrong. The emphasis on quick communication and logical responses has provided some of the cornerstones of today's arguments.

Imagine having an argument in which you made a logical statement, the other person made a logical statement, and then you chose between them. It would be a completely foreign (and probably not very effective) style of resolving a disagreement. Instead, thanks to the teachings of Socrates, Plato, and Aristotle, arguments in Ancient Greece evolved with a focus on communication and response. This brought arguments significantly closer to where they are today. That's why, if you and your significant other are fighting about milk, you each don't just make one statement about why you are right and then move on.

Lincoln

Being a great debater doesn't mean that you win all the time. For another lesson in arguing, we'll take a big step forward to the 1800s, when Abraham Lincoln was becoming known as one of the most influential debaters in history. Among his greatest accomplishments were the Lincoln-Douglas Debates in 1858. In these debates, Lincoln demonstrated that he was truly a master of arguments, although in the end, he did not win the election that the debates preceded.

Lincoln's specialty was the rebuttal. He was excellent at finding the problems with his opponent's logic and pointing them out. He also laid out rhetorical traps for his opponent, asking questions with no good answer. Finally, Lincoln didn't shy away from humor and cutting wit. He made direct attacks on his opponent.

In a debate in 1836, Lincoln responded to a question about his age by saying, "I would rather die now than, like the gentleman [meaning his opponent], see the day that I would change my politics for an office worth three thousand dollars a year." [11] Lincoln had an answer for everything, an answer which usually made his opponent look bad.

In the tradition of Aristotle, Lincoln thrived on quick discourse full of rebuttals and challenges. His legacy of arguments is also powerful because it paved the way for a change of public opinion on slavery – and its eventual abolition. Even a single argument, when done right, can change the world.

Mohandas Gandhi

When thinking about arguments, Gandhi probably isn't the first historical figure you think of. Right? After all, he espoused a nonviolent lifestyle and spent much of his time avoiding fights. However, Gandhi has a very essential lesson to teach us about arguments – that sometimes, the best argument is the one you don't have.

After seeing the discrimination faced by people of color in South Africa in the early 1900s, Gandhi developed and began to teach the concept of satyagraha ("truth and firmness"), also known as passive resistance. In 1914, Gandhi brought passive resistance to India, where he opposed the colonialists and pushed for India's independence. One of Gandhi's most famous quotes is, "An eye for an eye ends up making the whole world blind" – in other words, arguments based on vengeance are doomed to failure. [12]

Gandhi knew an important lesson that we often forget today. Great rhetoric and excellent facts aren't always enough to win an argument, especially when your opponent seems unreasonable. Instead, success can also come from taking a step back and carefully choosing the time, place, and method of your argument.

Today's Great Debates

Today's world is full of amazing arguers, too. From prominent politicians to promising high school students, these people are building on the legacy of those that came before every day. Even the slightest argument between family members still benefits from the rich history of arguing throughout the world.

What lessons can the arguers of the past teach the arguers of today? What concrete lessons can we draw from the people that came before us? Here is a brief list of the qualities that the world's greatest arguers have in common.

1. Logic - A reasoned, logical structure is the core of every argument. Someone's argument, whatever their opinion, will only be convincing if it is logical and the audience understands that logic.

2. Facts - In a world where not everything you read or hear is factual, well-researched facts make an argument believable. If you can produce accurate facts with trustworthy sources, people stop to listen.

3. Rebuttals - Just like Lincoln in his famous debates or Aristotle in his, any good arguer needs to be able to respond quickly and convincingly to his opponents' points.

4. Understanding of yourself and your opponent. No matter how good your logic is, you can't win without

understanding both your own strengths and weaknesses and those of your opponents.

5. Wisdom to decide which arguments to have – and when to have them. As Gandhi showed, sometimes the best arguments are the ones that don't happen or that happen in ways you might not expect.

When you look at today's best arguers, you can see these traits as clearly as ever. Think back to the last time that you listened to someone speak and felt convinced by what they were saying. It can be anyone: a politician, social media influencer, businessperson, or even a member of your own family. What did they say or do that convinced you to agree with them? Chances are, they drew on at least a few of the common characteristics above.

Action Steps

Begin by reflecting on your list of real-life arguments from the first chapter. Which common characteristics (logic, facts, rebuttals, knowledge of yourself and others, and wisdom to choose your arguments) do you see in yourself? Perhaps you usually use great facts and logic but struggle more with rebuttals. Or maybe you do well with understanding yourself and choosing arguments but tend to get flustered when it comes to logic. Once you know which characteristics you are already good at, you'll know which ones you need to focus on more in upcoming chapters.

Think also about your own idols of arguing. Maybe it's one of the historical figures in this chapter. Maybe it's someone you know in real life or someone you've read about or watched speak. Either way, study how they make their points. Do they use some of the common characteristics? Do they have some strategies that make them particularly convincing? As you continue through this book, keep those idols in mind. And when it comes to your own arguments, try to draw on their strengths.

In the next chapter, we'll look at the first two common characteristics: logic and facts. How can you make sure that both you and your conversation partner are using sound logic and accurate facts? And what are the most common ways that logic and facts can be stretched until they no longer make sense?

Chapter Summary

- Arguments are embedded in human history. Almost every ancient civilization had some tradition of arguing, although the arguments occurred at different times and places.
- Over time, arguments have evolved to become more complex and more focused on rebuttals and personal credibility.
- The best arguers, both past and present, share certain common characteristics. These include logic, facts, rebuttals, understanding of yourself

and others, and wisdom to choose your arguments.

3

THE CASE OF THE TECH-SAVVY SPINACH

S pinach can now send emails.

When a friend of mine told me this during a casual conversation, I was surprised – and immediately suspicious. After all, it hardly seems factual or logical that a vegetable could now be better at using the Internet better than my grandfather. So, I did a little research. Quickly, I found an article with the headline: "Scientists have taught spinach to send emails and it could warn us about climate change." [1] The article linked to a study with a slightly less catchy name: "Nitroaromatic detection and infrared communication from wild-type plants using plant nanobionics." [2]

It turns out that spinach isn't really sending emails, although it's a little closer than you might think. With some special implants, spinach plants can send out a fluorescent signal when they come into contact with certain chemicals. This signal is then picked up by a nearby camera, which sends the information to researchers. [3] It's false to say that spinach is sending emails, but it is true that the spinach is communicating in a way. Of course, the journalists behind the article weren't lying or even using incorrect facts. Still, some truth was definitely twisted in the creation of the headline.

What does tech-savvy spinach have to do with arguments? Everything. As we discussed in the last chapter, facts and logic are two important foundations of your argument. With facts and logic on your side, you can create a compelling argument about almost anything. Unfortunately, though, drawing logical conclusions from good evidence still doesn't guarantee that you'll have an accurate argument. When logic is stretched too far, you get emailing spinach.

How can you tell if your logic is really logical? How do you know if your facts are trustworthy? And equally important, how can you determine if the person you're arguing with is basing their statements on flawed logic or sketchy facts?

Logic And Logical Fallacies – Why Things Sound True When They Aren't

In the first chapter, we discussed a few different types of arguments, including deductive, inductive, and abductive. These types of arguments are based on logical strategies with the same name. For a quick review, inductive reasoning begins with a main statement that is applied to different examples. This could be, for instance: all pet turtles are green. My turtle is a pet, so she must be green. [4]

Deductive reasoning, on the other hand, starts with observations and draws a conclusion from there, i.e., my turtle is green and so is my coworker's pet turtle. So, all pet turtles must be green. [5]

Finally, abductive reasoning uses the facts that are available to find the most likely conclusion, i.e., my turtle is usually green, but now she is pink. My three-year-old's hands are also pink. My three-year-old probably painted the turtle. [6]

These styles of logical reasoning all seem to make sense. Unfortunately, just because a statement is logical or has some basis in facts doesn't necessarily mean that it's true. Let's dive into how logic can go wrong through logical fallacies, or common errors in the logical process. There are many possible fallacies but we'll discuss the eleven most common ones here.

1. Slippery Slope - In this fallacy, you assume that one event will lead to a series of other events, one of which is generally very undesirable. This might be, "The government shouldn't let anyone home-school their kids because, eventually, no kids will go to school, and we'll have a completely uneducated generation."

2. Hasty Generalization - This fallacy involves drawing a conclusion based on limited or biased evidence. If you're

making a hasty generalization, you might say, "Everyone from Vermont is really athletic. I met a person from there who runs marathons."

3. False Causality - In this fallacy, you assume that because one event happened after another, the second event must have caused the first. For instance, "I drank a bottle of water, and now I'm sick, so the bottle of water must have been tainted with something."

4. Ad Hominem - Ad hominem fallacies criticize an idea based on the person who gave it instead of based on some flaw in the idea. This kind of fallacy is very common in politics. It might be, "Mark spends a lot of money on online video games, so clearly he isn't fit to give anyone advice on budgeting."

5. Straw Man - Straw man fallacies attack a different position than the one being stated by the opponent. For instance, you might say, "I think we should try to reduce our environmental impact by printing double-sided." Using the straw man fallacy, your opponent might reply, "Ha, they think we can save the whole world by using a tiny bit less paper."

6. Appeal to Ignorance - In this fallacy, you assume that something must be true because it hasn't been proven false (or vice versa). For instance: "No one has been able to prove that Lucy doesn't have a secret stash of chocolate in her desk, so it must be true that she does."

7. False Dilemma - With a false dilemma, it seems like there are only two possible options, both of which are

usually extreme. An example of a false dilemma could be, "Either you love dogs, or you hate them."

8. Circular Arguments - Circular arguments present both the claim and the evidence together. For example, "All citizens have the right to vote because that is their right."

9. Sunk Cost - In a sunk cost fallacy, you continue to do something because you've already put effort into it, even if the other option might be more beneficial. For instance, you might say, "I bought tickets for the concert and asked for time off work already, so I'll go to the concert even though it's raining and I'm sick and it will definitely be miserable."

10. Bandwagon - A bandwagon fallacy assumes that something must be right or good because several people are doing it. For instance, "Everyone I know is voting for that politician, so he must be the best one."

11. False Equivalence - Our last fallacy is false equivalence, in which two things are stated to be the same, even if they aren't. For instance, "broccoli is green and so is some candy, so candy is as healthy as broccoli." [7]

If we take another look at the emailing spinach, we'll quickly find that the journalists were using false equivalence. The spinach was sending fluorescent signals to a computer, which is basically the same as emailing. Right? Not quite. That doesn't mean that the science is any less true or fascinating; it simply means that something went wrong logically when the article was written.

Most fallacies happen accidentally, often without our noticing them. I know I'm guilty of more than a few fallacies. Throughout the day, I might find myself thinking: "I ran slower than usual today, so now I'll never be a good athlete." Or: "I already watched half of this movie, so I should just finish the whole thing even though it's terrible." Or even: "Vanilla ice cream is boring because it just is."

That's alright. The first step in improving your logic is recognizing how it can go wrong. Next time you're having an argument, or even just going about your day, think carefully about how you and the people around you are making points. If you find yourself going down the path of a logical fallacy, step back for a moment and consider how you might be able to think about things differently.

Critical Thinking In Arguments

Recognizing logical fallacies in yourself is one thing. So is recognizing when you might be skirting around the truth or drawing on less-than-true evidence. It's much more difficult, though, to recognize when other people are using sketchy evidence or shaky logic, especially so when those people are experts (or at least appear to be). How can you think critically about what you are reading or hearing in a world where the truth can be hard to find?

Critical thinking is the ability to think clearly and logically about what you are reading, hearing, or seeing. [8] The concept is simple. Luckily, so is increasing your ability to think critically. There are three simple steps for improving your critical thinking, which we'll look at now.

The first part of critical thinking is to come with an open mind. If you start reading a book, watching a speech, or, most importantly, participating in an argument when you are certain that what you're about to hear is fallacious, you won't be able to analyze what's going on properly. Instead, keep your opinions in mind but be open to learning something contradictory.

Next, ask questions. In an argument, you have an advantage because you can question your partner directly about what you want to know. On the other hand, if you're conducting research by reading or listening, it's more likely that you'll need to write down your questions and look them up later. It's vital to understand where your conversation partner is getting their information, why they believe what they do, and what their responses are to potential problems in their theory. Without asking questions, you might miss the point that the other person is trying to make.

Finally, evaluate what you are learning along with what you already know. Maybe one person you're talking to says that coffee prevents cancer. Another responds that this is wrong: coffee actually causes cancer. Assuming you aren't sure which one is right, you can consider what you do know about coffee and cancer. You might remember that asbestos, a material that causes cancer, was banned in the United States, and removed from old buildings. Cigarettes also have warnings about their dangerous effects. So, if coffee caused cancer, there would probably be warnings about it, or it would be banned.

On the other hand, you know things that reduce the risk of cancer generally involve removing something that might cause cancer, such as protecting your skin from the sun, eating a balanced diet, and reducing tobacco or alcohol use. [9] So, drinking more coffee, which means adding something to your lifestyle, is not likely to prevent cancer.

Using logical evaluation based on what you know, you can determine that both statements are probably wrong. Of course, you shouldn't rely on logic alone. Using a reliable source such as a clinic or cancer research website, you should also look up coffee's effect on cancer. If you do, you'll learn that there is no definitive evidence that coffee either causes or prevents cancer. [10]

With these three steps (keeping an open mind, asking questions, and evaluating logically based on existing knowledge) you can think more critically about any argument you are having, book you are reading, or television program you are watching. The most important component of critical thinking is asking the right questions, which can also be the hardest part. How do you know which questions will get the right information?

"I Really Want To Know" – How To Ask The Right Questions

Good questions are important, not just in an argument, but in any situation. In fact, one of the most common conversational complaints is that people don't ask enough questions, whether the situation is a first date, a work interview, or a heated argument. So, how do questions work in our daily lives? And why do some work better than others in certain situations?

There are four different types of questions that are asked most often. These are mirror, introductory, full-switch, and follow-up questions. [11] An introductory question opens a conversation, such as asking "How are you?" or "Have you met Tiffany before?" A mirror question repeats the question you were just asked, such as replying "I'm fine, how are you?" or "I'm not sure, have you met Tiffany?" A full-switch question completely changes the topic of the conversation, such as replying, "I do know Tiffany. Hey, do you like bowling?" Finally, a follow-up question builds on what was said, such as asking, "I have met Tiffany. Why do you ask?"

So, which type of questions should you be asking? Any of the four types can be useful at times, but follow-up questions tend to bring the best results in arguments. In conversations with follow-up questions, people tend to feel more heard and talk for longer. [12] In arguments, follow-up questions not only show that you are listening but also that you are trying your best to understand the other person's point of view.

As well as asking follow-up questions, another strategy for good questions is to keep questions open-ended when possible. Questions that can only be answered with yes or no tend to make answerers feel like they are being backed into a corner. [13]If you ask, for instance, "Do you think Tiffany is great or not?" the other person might struggle to answer if they think Tiffany is nice but maybe not 'great.' Worse, they can get defensive, saying something like, "What? Why are you asking? I don't care about Tiffany." A better strategy is to ask, "What do you think of Tiffany?" leaving the question open to a wider range of answers.

Next, sequence your questions correctly. If you begin a conversation by asking, "What's your biggest regret?" you probably won't get an honest answer. Instead, you can start with simple questions about memories, goals, and life satisfaction before moving on to the deeper and more sensitive questions. That will enable you to get a more honest and thoughtful answer, because the person will feel more comfortable and more in the correct mindset to answer.

Similarly, questions should be ordered carefully to prevent biases. In one study, some participants were asked first, "How satisfied are you with your life?" then "How satisfied are you with your marriage?" In this study, the answers were highly correlated (i.e., people were either satisfied or not satisfied with both equally). Other participants were asked the questions in reverse order, marriage and then life, and the answers were no longer very correlated (i.e., people might be happy with one and unhappy with the other). [14] This is because, in the first group, the questions were presented as related (marriage was seen as a subset of life). In everyday conversation, this means that you might want to be careful about asking, for instance, "Did you read the article about the man getting attacked by his pet dog?" followed by, "Do you want to get a dog?"

Finally, use the right tone. When presented with questions in a serious way, people are less likely to answer deeply and honestly than when asked questions in a light-hearted and casual way. [15] Of course, in an argument, your tone tends to be more serious than happy-go-lucky. That's alright. You can still try to keep your questions friendly and modify your phrasing. Questions like "Where did you learn about this?" will get better answers than "Who on earth told you that nonsense?"

In short, you can ask better questions using four strategies. First, favor follow-up questions. Second, keep your questions open-ended when possible. Third, sequence your questions from less to more sensitive. And fourth, use a friendly and polite tone.

Building A Better Argument

Bringing everything together, how do you build a better argument? Simply ask good questions, just like we discussed above, and come with an open mind and a willingness to listen and, if convinced, change your opinion. Also, make your arguments meaningful. Bring your genuine thoughts, questions, and research to the table.

Of course, all this is much easier said than done. When you're calm, collected, and relaxed, as you hopefully are when reading this book, it seems very straightforward to just be open-minded and ask good questions. In the heat of an argument, things might look different. So, here is the practical list of Dos and Don'ts in arguments.

- Do: Choose the right place. If someone has ever started an argument with you in public after a long day of work, you know what I'm talking about. For a good argument, make sure that both you and the person you're talking to start calm, rested, and in a comfortable private location.
- Don't: Start an argument you can't finish. If you or the other person need to leave for work, get to sleep, or finish a project, it's not the right time. You'll either be late, rush to end the argument, or walk away in the middle with bad feelings on both sides.
- Do: Have a clear goal in mind. Start your argument with, for instance, the agenda to resolve an issue you've been having with the other person or to agree on a mutually important topic.

- Don't: Make that goal 'winning.' If you have an argument with the sole agenda of convincing the other person that they are completely wrong and you are completely right, you've already lost.
- Do: Ask lots of questions. More important than asking the perfect question is asking a lot of questions. In this case, it really is quantity over quality. You don't want to end the conversation having missed something important just because you were too busy thinking of what to ask.
- Don't: Ask trap questions. Trying to lead your partner to a logical conclusion via questions is okay. Trying to ask questions that you know will create a bad situation isn't. This includes questions designed to make the other person feel bad or look foolish.
- Do: Look for a middle ground between your opinion and your conversation partner's opinion. Even if this is something relatively minor, finding agreement can help move things forward and make both sides feel more open.
- Don't: Say things you don't believe just to end the argument. If you say you agree or understand, even when you don't, you'll run into more trouble later than if you end the argument by agreeing to disagree.
- Do: Summarize for understanding. At the end of an argument or at key points, restate the other person's point. This could look like, "It sounds like you agree that we should try to eat more

healthily, but that you're worried about the additional cost and preparation time. Is that right?"

With these Dos and Don'ts in mind, you can build the kind of argument that will be productive and end in a better place than it starts for both you and the person you're talking to.

Action Steps

Start with a hunt for logical fallacies. The more you train yourself to recognize them in the world around you, the more you'll be able to recognize them in yourself and the people you're arguing with. Over the next few days, keep your eyes open as you read, watch television, and talk to people. Do you notice a certain reporter on the news tends to use the slippery slope fallacy? Does one of your coworkers often end up in a sunk cost fallacy? Do you sometimes find yourself in a false dilemma fallacy? Keep training yourself to look for these issues and, over time, you'll find your logical skills increasing.

Next, practice asking good questions. As we discussed, these could be open-ended and follow-up questions asked in the right tone and the right order. The important thing, though, is to find your own method for asking good questions. The best way to do this is to use the Spaghetti on the Wall method. The Spaghetti on the Wall method simply means trying as many different things as you can to see what will work best, like throwing spaghetti at the wall to see if it's cooked (in which case it will stick). When it comes to questions, this means asking questions, as many as you can think of, to as many people as you find yourself talking to. Eventually, you'll notice patterns in the questions that get the best answers.

Finally, create your own list of argument Dos and Don'ts. Start with the list above and add to it. Maybe you should never argue with your spouse on a Saturday because that's your day to relax. Maybe you should always prepare questions and points ahead of time before arguing with your boss. Or maybe you should be careful when arguing about a certain topic, such as politics, because it is important to you, and you tend to get upset. Keep your list on hand and add to it (or remove things) based on how your arguments go. In the end, you'll have a cheat sheet on how to argue well.

Spinach can send emails. At the beginning of this chapter, we learned that, even though this statement is based on real research, it isn't strictly true. And, we learned how to create a better argument to disprove this statement or any other.

What if you hear someone in your family or at work make the spinach claim, though? Will you dive into an argument, using good questions, logic, and helpful rules to prove that spinach isn't actually hopping onto the internet? Or will you let the statement slide, going back to what you were doing with nothing more than a quiet shake of your head?

Let's dive deeper into how humans decide to start or avoid an argument – and how you can decide better which arguments are worth having.

Chapter Summary

- Most people are guilty of making logical fallacies – errors in the logical process that make something sound true, even if it isn't.
- You can often tell if something is true or false through critical thinking. This means listening with an open mind, asking good questions, and comparing what you hear with what you already know.
- Asking good questions means asking questions that follow up on what was said, that are open-ended, in the right order, and in the right tone. However, the most important thing is to ask lots of questions.
- When arguing, follow certain Dos and Don'ts, such as bringing an open mind, choosing the right place, and looking for common ground.

4

STUCK IN THE MIDDLE WITH YOU

I n one popular American television show, The Big Bang Theory, a woman climbs out of a restaurant window to avoid arguing with her boyfriend. The boyfriend, eager to resolve their disagreement, follows her to the parking lot to continue the conversation. Of course, neither is happy with how the argument goes – they are on completely different pages about if it's an argument worth having.

Although this is an extreme example, it is reflected in how we really interact with each other. Often, people disagree about whether arguing is fun or terrible. They make decisions about whether or not to argue based on both good and sketchy reasoning. And sometimes, they make the wrong decision and regret either having or walking away from an argument.

In this chapter, we'll look at two of the most important questions when it comes to arguments. Why do we choose to engage in the arguments that we do? And how can we make better decisions about which arguments to join?

Love It Or Hate It

Some people thrive when engaging in an argument and even seek them out. Others, however, avoid arguments at any cost. Most of us are somewhere in the middle. We choose to engage in the arguments that are important to us or that we think we can win and avoid the arguments that seem unproductive or pointless. Or at least, we think we do. Often, the processes that lead us to join or avoid an argument are subconscious and influenced by more factors than just the situation at hand.

There are many good reasons to start or join an argument. Arguments can settle a disagreement, widen your thinking, or move your research on a topic forward. [1] To an individual, arguments help us understand what we believe and help us explain our beliefs to others. Meanwhile, on a societal level, arguments help us understand larger truths and develop policies. [2] Often, arguments start with excellent intentions of resolving issues or finding the truth. People who are driven by the search for knowledge and who enjoy analytical and rational thought tend to choose arguments more often than others do. [3] This is part of why scientists and philosophers spend much of their careers arguing.

Unfortunately, there are also unproductive reasons to start an argument. One is trying to prove that you are rational and correct at any cost. This can lead to a confirmation bias, in which you look for information that supports your conclusion instead of looking for the truth. [4] It can also lead to spending all your mental energy on trying to use logic to win instead of trying to understand the other person's point.

Another problematic reason to start an argument is lack of sleep. People who sleep less argue more – and have worse results when they do. [5] This is because tired brains are not as logical and tend to be on a shorter fuse. Just think of the last time you didn't get enough sleep and found everything more annoying than usual.

Finally, people tend to start arguments when they perceive a power imbalance, such as when a co-worker has a lot of power but doesn't seem to be using it well. [6] Imagine that your co-worker has been asked to review your work, but instead of being helpful, they are nitpicky. At the time, you might just accept this because you don't feel powerful enough to fight back. Later in the kitchen, though, you might start an argument with your coworker about the dishes to vent the frustration you are feeling with them.

What does all this mean for people who tend to choose argument over avoidance? It simply means that when you feel the pull to join or start an argument, you should take a moment to think over your motivations. Are you hoping to find truth, compromise, or simply an interesting debate? Do you want to widen your horizons? Are you hoping to solve a mutual problem? Or are you interested only in winning or establishing a new power dynamic?

Similarly, when someone opens an argument with you, think about their reasons and make sure that you're on the same page. If they are tired, upset, or belligerent, they may start an argument for the wrong reasons. In this case, it's best to walk away and plan to discuss the topic later, if needed.

In fact, walking away because you or your conversation partner isn't ready for a productive debate is the first and best reason to avoid arguments. If you can't see a positive solution to an argument, the argument has turned into a fight, or the time and place are wrong, choosing not to argue is the best option for you and the other person.

For instance, in a study of nurses, researchers found that conflict in the hospital leads to worse conditions for patients and sometimes poor decision-making. [7] In some cases, particularly in work environments or high-stakes situations, any decision is better than a drawn-out argument. So, if you step away from an argument because a solution is more important than being right, that's also a good decision.

On the other hand, there are harmful reasons to step away from an argument. Some people with low self-esteem tend to avoid arguments because they feel that the other person's needs and opinions are more valuable than their own. This means that they will usually concede or reach a "compromise" that only attends to the other person's needs, not their own. [8] While this is a quick way to end an argument, it usually leads to bad feelings and unresolved issues.

Imagine you are having an argument with your significant other about whose turn it is to pick up the kids from school. Not wanting to argue, you agree to go, even though you have a lot of work to do and have been picking the kids up almost every day. Now, when you do go to the school pick-up, you might feel unhappy and resentful that you have to do work you don't have time for.

Similarly, some people choose not to argue because of power imbalances (exactly the opposite of people who choose *to* argue because of power imbalances). [9] This is especially common in the workplace or in families. It can lead to people going along with decisions that they know are wrong just to avoid getting into an argument. This can have relatively small effects: perhaps you see a movie you don't like and are frustrated for a few hours, but move on quickly. It can also be much more impactful, though: maybe you go along with an incorrect decision at work because you don't feel comfortable speaking up and your company loses profits.

So, just as you examine your reasoning before starting an argument, it's important to examine your reasoning before avoiding one. Are you choosing not to argue because the other person isn't in the right mindset? Are you avoiding an argument because a decision is better than no decision? Or are you avoiding an argument because you are worried about speaking up?

In short, some people prefer to argue while others prefer to walk away. Both can be good strategies when used in the right circumstances, but both can be problematic, too. How can you train yourself to make the right decision about whether or not to join an argument?

Look Both Ways – The Pros And Cons Of Arguing

Before you join an argument, take a moment to assess both the benefits and drawbacks of engaging in this particular argument. Below, you'll find a checklist of conditions necessary for a productive argument. If these conditions are not met, you are better off walking away.

- You and the other person are both arguing for the right reasons
- You and the other person agree on the topic of the argument
- You have enough time to finish the argument
- You are in a comfortable and private location
- You have something to gain by arguing, such as solving a problem, finding the truth, or reaching a compromise

If this is all true, you are probably better off arguing. On the other hand, if one or more of these factors are missing, you will probably get better results by setting the argument aside and coming back to it later and with better conditions, if necessary.

How should you walk away from an argument if it isn't going to go well? It depends a lot on the situation and the person. If a stranger or acquaintance is trying to start an argument with you, you can say something along the lines of "I don't feel comfortable discussing this at the moment" or simply change the topic.

In work or home environments, it can be more difficult. Start by acknowledging the other person's point of view, such as by saying, "I understand why you are worried about my decisions on this project." Then explain why you don't want to engage in an argument now, "Since the project is due tomorrow, I don't think we have enough time for major changes." Finally, offer a way to move forward together, "On the next project, let's have a meeting early on so that we can exchange ideas and make sure we're both happy with it."

The same strategy works with disputes among family and friends, too. Perhaps you can tell your spouse, "I see why you're worried about spending money on restaurants. We should discuss that, but right now it's getting late, and we both need to get to work. How about we continue this discussion this evening?"

When walking away from an argument, be sure not to suggest that you think the argument isn't worth having. If someone is bringing up a topic for discussion with you, that means that it is important to them. So, no matter how small it seems to you, it's worth taking the time to discuss the topic when the circumstances are right.

On the other hand, what happens if someone is trying to avoid an argument that you know is necessary? Of course, following someone around demanding to engage in an argument is very counterproductive. Instead, focus on creating a comfortable space for arguing, following the Dos and Don'ts in the last chapter. When they feel safe and heard, people are more likely to engage in an argument, even if they were initially reluctant. It can also help to choose a different, better time and/or place to have the argument.

Win Or Lose

In this chapter, we discussed many good and bad reasons to start an argument. It's important to note, however, that "winning" wasn't listed among the good reasons. So often, we start arguments with the goal of winning. And almost as often, this leads to problems. If two people in an argument will only end the argument when they win, and winning means convincing the other person of your opinion completely, the argument will never end.

Instead, let's look at the concept of winning an argument a little differently. Conventional wisdom suggests that winning an argument means convincing the other person of your opinion, to the point that they drop their original stance. Starting an argument with this goal is almost always a bad decision.

Instead, winning an argument can mean reaching a positive conclusion. This could mean that one person changes their opinion. However, it could also mean that both parties decide to agree to disagree. It could mean that they reach a mutually beneficial compromise. It could even mean that they decide they were both wrong. As long as the argument ends with both parties feeling positive and agreeing on something (even if that's just that they still disagree), you can consider the argument "won."

Action Steps

Begin by determining whether you are the kind of person who gravitates toward arguments, avoids them, or is somewhere in between. You can review the list of arguments from Chapter One, or simply observe the arguments that you had and didn't have in the last week or so. For you personally, why do you enjoy or dislike arguing? When do you regret having or not having an argument? What kinds of arguments usually end with the best results?

Next, apply your findings. If you discover that you often regret arguing with your father-in-law, because he only cares about winning and tends to get belligerent, try some of the above strategies to avoid arguing with him next time. On the other hand, if you usually regret not arguing with your boss when she asks you to take on too much work, see if you can respectfully disagree with her next time.

Arguments are necessary in our society for many reasons, but they only give positive results in the right circumstances. With all this in mind, you can avoid either climbing out the window or chasing someone who clearly doesn't want to argue. You can choose more effectively when you want to argue and who you want to argue with.

What happens, though, when the argument occurs within your own mind, between what you are learning and your existing worldview? In the next chapter, we'll look at how the mind processes new information and how we can have better arguments with ourselves.

Chapter Summary

- People choose to argue for positive reasons, such as finding a solution, resolving a disagreement, or expanding their horizons.
- People also choose to argue for negative reasons, such as lack of sleep, power imbalances, or a need to be right.
- People choose not to argue for positive reasons, for instance, because they or the other person are not in the right mood, or because any solution is better than no solution.
- People also choose not to argue for negative reasons, such as low self-esteem or uneven power dynamics.
- Before starting an argument, make sure that you have the right reasons for doing so.
- Additionally, be sure that you and your partner agree on the topic of the argument, that you're

in a good place with enough time, and that you have something to gain by arguing.

- Finally, focus on "winning" an argument more broadly. Winning doesn't mean changing the other person's opinion, but instead reaching a positive conclusion.

5

BELIEVE IT OR NOT

T ake a moment to look at the image below. Are the long lines in the picture parallel?

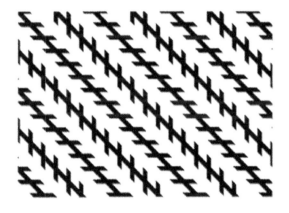

1

Maybe you've seen this illusion before, or maybe you're naturally skeptical of optical illusions, and you know that the lines are, in fact, parallel. Even so, it's a little hard to believe, right? Because of the smaller lines crossing the long lines at an angle, the long lines appear to be slanted toward each other. Even though you know that the lines aren't slanted at all, you might still struggle to see it. That's because your conscious brain tells you that the lines are parallel, but another part of your brain tells you that this isn't possible.

Optical illusions are one of the most well-known tricks that our brains play on us, but they aren't the only ones. Even when you do your best to be neutral and see things as they really are, you still view the world through the lens of your past experiences and knowledge. In this chapter, we'll discuss the mental tricks that our minds play on us and how to get past them to think more clearly.

Mental Models

When you read or hear a new piece of information, the first thing that your brain does is try to fit that information into your mental model. [2] A mental model sounds complicated, but it's just the way that your mind organizes information about different topics. It's like a shelving unit in your brain.

Practically, imagine your mental model of a dog. As a child, you learn about dogs: they bark, they have four legs, and they are often kept as pets. As a teenager, you might get your own dog and add more information to your mental model, for instance, that dogs don't like to go for walks in the rain and that they enjoy being scratched on the stomach. Finally, if you study to become a veterinarian as an adult, you'll add information about a dog's anatomy and physiology to your mental model.

Often, new information fits neatly into your mental model. If your friend shows you a picture of their dog and tells you how cute and fluffy the dog is, you'll nod along without question because this fits with what you already know. Meanwhile, you'll add more information to your mental model about how nice dogs are.

Let's say, though, that your friend instead tells you that they hate dogs. Dogs are terrible! They chase people, sometimes bite, and slobber all over everything. Suddenly, your brain is confused. This new information that dogs are terrible doesn't fit anywhere into your mental model. This triggers your brain to tell you that your friend must be wrong – after all, your whole mental model is built based on the assumption that dogs are great.

This same process happens in your mind whenever you hear information that doesn't fit the mental model you've built. In response, you might start an argument, disregard the information, or adjust your mental model to include a new section on how dogs are sometimes not so friendly. It's similar to what happens if your spouse brings home an enormous new household appliance that you have no room for. You can either argue about it, throw it away when your spouse isn't looking, or move things around until you find a place for it.

Unfortunately, as useful as mental models are for helping us learn and store information, they can undermine our ability to argue effectively. [3] We all have a wealth of information that backs up our points of view. Because of our existing opinions, we sometimes struggle to change and expand our mental models when presented with information that doesn't fit with what we already know. This is most difficult when you are just starting to learn about a topic because your brain wants to believe that it has all the information – even when it doesn't. This can trigger a lot of internal arguments between what you already know and what you're seeing or hearing.

Internal arguments often start when our mental models are challenged, but they can also start without any external prompting. This is the struggle between the conscious and subconscious mind. Your subconscious mind spurs reaction and instinct, while the conscious mind is your train of thought.[4] These two parts of your mind often argue with each other, because your logical mind tells you one thing, while your instincts tell you another. Imagine you wake up one morning with the plan to go jogging. Your conscious mind, the part that you control, tells you that you always feel better after exercise and you should just get up and go. Meanwhile, your unconscious mind, the part that happens behind the scenes, tells you that your bed is very warm and you should just sleep a little more. You can think of your subconscious mind as all the things you "just know," like that your bed is warm and that you like certain people or things. [5]

In real arguments, your conscious and subconscious play a role too. Your conscious mind might tell you to listen to the other person because they could have something interesting to say. Meanwhile, your subconscious mind might tell you that they must be wrong because you are always right. It could be the other way, too: your conscious mind might argue that this argument is important and worth having, while your subconscious mind tells you that you care too much about this person to argue with them.

Your subconscious mind also brings you instincts, which are vital for our survival. Instincts make you jerk your hand away when you touch something hot and hold onto something if you feel like you're going to fall. Unfortunately, instincts can also make it more difficult to process information correctly and accurately.

Instincts are often unhelpful when it comes to learning or arguing. If you come across a new fact that contradicts what you have learned before, your instincts tell you to just ignore it.

There are ten instincts that most influence our abilities to process new information correctly. These all happen internally, but once you know about them, you can start to see past them.

The 10 Instincts

1. The Gap Instinct - This is our instinct to divide things into two very different groups. You can think of it a little

like the false dilemma logical fallacy. These groups could be "us" and "them," or "right" and "wrong," when in fact, there's more in common between the groups than we think.

2. The Negativity Instinct - Our negativity instinct tells us that things are always getting worse. This is why we tend to believe bad news more than good (for instance, "hundreds of people die of a new disease" is more believable than "millions of people get sick and then recover").

3. The Straight Line Instinct - This instinct tells us that things will probably continue as they have until now – even though this doesn't usually happen in real life. We might assume, for instance, that a child who loves to say "no!" will be argumentative forever.

4. The Fear Instinct - Just like how we believe negative things more than positive ones, we tend to pay more attention to scary things. People are much more likely to click on the headline: "Woman murdered in sleep!" than "Billions of people sleep peacefully every night." This is also why politicians tend to use frightening language in their campaign speeches.

5. The Size Instinct - This is our instinct to overestimate things, especially negative ones. For instance, you might overestimate the amount of work you have to do or the number of bad days you've had this year.

6. The Generalization Instinct - We often generalize things, especially things we don't know much about. One

bad burrito might make you avoid Mexican food for years, especially if it's the first burrito you have ever tried.

7. The Destiny Instinct - This is the instinct that people's innate characteristics or past experiences define their future. We might say that someone won the lottery because they deserved it or lost their job because they weren't working hard, even if the real reason is more complicated.

8. The Single Perspective Instinct - This is our instinct to view things only from one perspective and to gain more and more information that fits that perspective. If you have a strong political view, for instance, you may watch the news and talk to people with the same view.

9. The Blame Instinct - The Blame Instinct pushes us to find one clear reason why something happened. Maybe your picnic was ruined by rain because your friend forgot to check the forecast, or maybe Lucy got sick because she didn't wash her hands yesterday.

10. The Urgency Instinct - This is our tendency to act right away, especially when things look bad. This instinct amplifies our other instincts because it takes away the time to consider alternatives. This is why we might buy things on sale that we wouldn't otherwise want.[6]

In short, our brains aren't perfect at processing information. Even when trying to be perfectly neutral, we have biases and incorrect classifications about any new piece of information. However, this doesn't mean we're helpless against our biases and instincts. With awareness and attention, we can more clearly think through internal arguments.

Clear Thoughts, Clear Actions

Changing how your brain processes new information isn't easy. After all, we think the way we do for a good reason. Our mental models keep information organized so that we can find and apply it again and again. Our subconscious mind helps keep us safe by encouraging us to stay where things are familiar. And our instincts let us process information and act quickly.

The simple answer for changing these processes is to be aware of them. This is similar to logical fallacies. Once you know how logic can go wrong, you'll be on the lookout and more able to correct fallacies you find in yourself. In the same way, when you're aware of improper instincts or incorrect processing, you'll be more able to stop yourself and try a better way.

Whenever you encounter new information, the best thing to do is to think about your assumptions and ask yourself why you feel that way. Let's say you read an article which explains that there are more dog bites in your city than ever before. You'll probably have thoughts about this right away. For some people, this confirms what they already know about dogs: that they are mean creatures who bite people. For others, it goes against everything they know about dogs: they are sweet and gentle creatures who would never harm someone without provocation. Either way, this reaction is your mental model and your instincts interacting with the new information. Think carefully about why you feel the way you do. Do you reject the article because it doesn't fit with what you already know? Or do you believe it just because it plays into your fears, even if there isn't enough proof?

Beyond your personal feelings, make sure to look at the facts of the article clearly. Let's say that the article states that there were 50% more dog bites in your city this year than last year. This sounds huge, but it isn't necessarily true, even though it plays into our size instincts. Maybe there were two dog bites last year, while this year there were three. Or maybe there were more dog bites this year, but also more dogs in the city overall, so really, there was a decrease in the percentage of bites per dog. The more you see the actual numbers behind statistics or stories, the more you can see the data clearly instead of listening to biases and instincts.

The most vital thing about thinking clearly is applying the same rigorous questioning to new information that fits with what you already know as you do with new information that doesn't. If you believe that dogs are the best animal in the world, you would probably see the 'dog bites' headline and immediately start looking for logical or factual issues in the article, just like I described above. But if you believe that dogs are mean anyway, you might see the headline, nod, and not look any further because you believe it. Clearly, logical thinking without biases means being skeptical of things that sound true, not just things that sound false.

You can also purposefully slow your thinking to prevent biases. We have two different ways of thinking: System 1 and System 2. [7] System 1 is the one we use most of the time and relies on intuition, emotion, and mental models. It's much faster. Unfortunately, System 1 is also more prone to errors. If you see a man stepping toward you wearing a police officer's uniform, System 1 will tell you that this is a policeman and that you should do what he says. It's when we're operating in System 1 that we struggle the most with bias and instinct.

System 2 is more rational, but it's also slower. System 2 engages when we carefully evaluate the information we receive, such as when studying for a test or trying to decide if something is true or false. System 2 can tell you that the man in the police officer's uniform is just wearing a Halloween costume and that you don't need to do what he says.

So, when you want to make sure that the information you're receiving is accurate without bias, consciously use System 2. This simply means slowing down and taking the time to consider the new information thoughtfully instead of rushing through and moving on to the next thing. You can activate System 2 by pausing after reading a paragraph to consider the information and ask yourself questions.

How does clear thinking play a role in arguments? The more clearly you are able to think about and process what you already know, the better you'll be at responding to new information, too. Let's say you're arguing about politics with a family member over the holidays. When they make some statements you disagree with about their favorite politicians, you can determine if they have any good points or if one or both of you is falling into a mental trap. You can also avoid jumping to conclusions when someone makes a controversial point. Clear thinking keeps you from believing what is easiest about others and yourself.

The most important thing to keep in mind when it comes to internal arguments and mental tricks is self-reflection. In the last section, we talked about using self-reflection to find out biases in the article about dog bites. This – finding biases and unhelpful instincts – is one of the most important functions of self-reflection. The other is a reflection on arguments before and after joining them.

Mirror, Mirror

Our brains have trouble remembering arguments correctly. Before an argument, it might seem that arguing is the only possible way to resolve a situation. During an argument, you may think about all the other times you've argued with this person and how bad that makes you feel. And after an argument, you might think that you didn't make your case clearly enough and that you should have added a few other points.

In most cases, all of these thought patterns are incomplete. Yes, an argument might solve this issue, but there might also be a better way. Sure, you might have argued with this person a lot before, but that doesn't mean your relationship is all negative. And of course, you could have made your point better, but that's no reason to reopen the argument.

In order to argue better, try to reflect on your actions at each point of the arguing process. Why is it important to have this argument now? Why are you feeling so negatively about the person you're arguing with, even though they're someone you care about? And why do you find yourself wishing that you could have said something different?

Many of these common questions in self-reflection come back to our instincts – for instance, the gap instinct (you think the other person is making a more different point to yours when they aren't) and negativity instinct (when something frustrating happens, and it's hard to remember all the good). Try to correct these instincts when you discover them. If you find yourself thinking that the other person is making an irreconcilable point compared to yours, try to look for a middle ground and remember past compromises. If you find yourself feeling very negative about the other person, try to remember the good times you've had before and all the reasons why you care about this person.

Does all this mean that you can never have a good argument where your instincts are involved? No. It simply means that you should acknowledge your biases, instincts, and subconscious mental processes. And whenever possible, you should try to set these aside to have fairer, more factual, better arguments.

Action Steps

It's time to put your clear-thinking skills to use. Go online and find four articles from reputable news sources. These should be from major media outlets with editors and fact-checking. If you are unsure, you can look up major reliable news sources in your country.

Two of the articles you choose should instantly make sense to you. The topics should align with your interests and your current worldviews. The other two should seem improbable. The topic should be something you don't know much about or don't agree with.

Then, read all four articles one by one, slowly and methodically. Try to be just as logical and skeptical about the articles you agree with as the ones you don't. And do your best to find something in the articles you disagree with, even if it's relatively small, that does make sense to you.

After reading, reflect on your experience. Was it easy to poke holes in the articles that you disagreed with? Was it harder to find something that didn't make sense in the articles you did agree with? As well as helping you see mental processes in action, this exercise will help you strengthen your clear-thinking skills.

Like in the optical illusion at the beginning of the chapter, illusions exist at every level of our mental processing. Each new piece of information is processed, sometimes correctly and sometimes incorrectly. With practice, you can make your mental processes clearer and more accurate.

This becomes a little more difficult in the context of an actual argument with another person. How do the strategies you've learned play out when you're arguing with another person who may not be as logical or reasonable as you want them to be? In the next chapter, we'll take arguments into the real world and look at how we can better argue with the people we care about.

Chapter Summary

- When we get new information, we try to fit it into our mental model (a place in your mind where you store information on a certain topic).
- When it doesn't fit, we can become confused or reject the new information completely, even if it is accurate.
- There's also an internal argument between our conscious minds, which are our purposeful thoughts, and our unconscious minds, which run on instinct.
- Ten instincts affect data processing the most. These instincts make us focus on negative, scary,

familiar information that aligns with what we already believe.

- The best way to think more clearly about new information is to slow your thought process down and look for possible biases in your own mind.
- It's also important to reflect on arguments, as we may not always remember them correctly and may have instinctive biases about our arguments.

6

THE OTHER HALF OF THE ARGUMENT

You're ready to put everything into practice. An argument starts with your loved one and you feel good about it. The time is right. Your arguments are logical and thoughtful. You're ready to find a compromise and see both points of view.

Instead, everything spirals out of control. Your loved one isn't listening. They're using emotion and illogical arguments that sound completely unreasonable. Suddenly, both of you are raising your voices and slamming doors. What happened? Why do even the best-planned arguments fall apart in the real world? And most importantly, what can you do to argue better with the people around you?

Yell, Shout, Pout

Across cultures, ages, and topics, arguing people share a few common tendencies, like raising their voices. These tendencies are perfectly understandable. We raise our voices, for instance, because we want to be heard. Still, these tendencies can have a negative impact on your argument by distorting your point or making the other person feel unheard. Let's look at a few of the most common tendencies in arguing, why we do them, why they don't work, and what you can do instead.

Raised voices/yelling

Why we do it: To make sure that our points and feelings are heard, to get our frustrations across, or to vent anger.

Why it doesn't work: Raised voices or yelling can make us sound intimidating or out-of-control and can distract from the point we're trying to make.

What to do instead: If you find yourself starting to raise your voice, take a moment to step back and take a deep breath. Then lower your voice to a normal speaking volume.

What if someone else does it: Lower your own voice – if someone raises their voice and the other doesn't, it can often de-escalate the situation. If this doesn't work and the other person seems too frustrated to argue, ask for a small break.

Sarcasm

Why we do it: When faced with something illogical or frustrating, it can be easier to be sarcastic than to engage.

Why it doesn't work: Depending on the situation, a sarcastic tone makes it sound either like you're making fun of the other person or just not taking things seriously.

What to do instead: Figure out why you want to use sarcasm and address that problem instead. If the other person sounds completely illogical, try to get to the root of what they are saying or ask them to state it another way.

What if someone else does it: Address the sarcastic comment straightforwardly. If the other person says, "Oh, yeah, after a long day of work I'd just looove to do more chores," calmly reply, "I know you don't. Maybe we can find a time on the weekends to do work around the house."

Silence

Why we do it: Similar to sarcasm, it can be easier to just shut down than to face a confusing or frustrating argument.

Why it doesn't work: If you're silent, the other person won't know your opinion – and might not even know that you disagree. Alternatively, if you go quiet in the middle of an argument, it can seem like you aren't paying attention.

What to do instead: Take a moment to gather your thoughts, then say what you need to say. Even if it doesn't come out exactly right, it's better to say something than stay quiet.

What if someone else does it: First, give them some time to gather their thoughts – maybe they just need a few minutes to think about what to say. Then ask them plainly to talk to you. If they refuse, say, "Okay, let's take a break and come back to this when you're ready."

Reaching

Why we do it: Once you start arguing, it can be tempting to reach further back to find other annoyances and past issues.

Why it doesn't work: Not only does this drag the argument out longer and increase negative feelings from both sides, it distracts from the original topic of the argument and reduces the likelihood that it will get resolved.

What to do instead: If the argument brings up old feelings or issues, acknowledge that, but don't bring it into this argument.

What if someone else does it: Acknowledge what they brought up, then request that it be addressed later. i.e., "I know you were really upset when I was rude to your friend. I'm still sorry, but I don't think it's relevant to this conversation. Can we discuss it after this is resolved?"

Walking away

Why we do it: It can be easier to just remove yourself from an argument than listen to a contrary opinion that seems unreasonable.

Why it doesn't work: Although avoiding an argument can be a reasonable strategy, as we discussed in <u>Chapter Three</u>, walking away in the middle of an argument can lead to bad results. The other person might become angrier or even worried that you won't come back.

What to do instead: If you need to take a break from an argument, tell the other person clearly that you need a break but that you will be ready to continue the conversation at a certain time. Then stick to that.

What if someone else does it: Don't follow them – let them take the time away that they need. After the argument is resolved, though, ask them to let you know next time if they need a break and how long they need instead of walking away without saying anything.

<u>Hyperbole</u>

Why we do it: When we're upset, it can be tempting to emphasize the situation by using strong words. This includes phrases like "you always," or "you never," or even just "that's impossible" (if it is, indeed, possible).

Why it doesn't work: Using hyperbole can make the other person feel attacked or unheard. It can also undermine your own argument because it seems like your argument isn't strong enough on its own and needs to be exaggerated.

What to do instead: Keep your arguments focused on the facts of your argument. Instead of saying "you never clean the bathroom," say "I feel like I clean the bathroom more often than you do."

What if someone else does it: Don't try to fight back with contradictory examples. Instead, address what they are trying to say and offer a solution, if possible, "maybe we can work out a way to plan whose turn it is to clean the bathroom."

If you find that you have these tendencies during arguments, it's no reason to feel bad. There are understandable reasons why so many people do them. Even once you work on these tendencies in yourself, you're very likely to find other people who still raise their voices or go quiet. That's why this chapter is focused on how to argue with other people in the real world – even when they give in to less-than-helpful tendencies.

Emotion In Arguments

Many of the above tendencies are inspired by strong emotions, often anger. In general, using emotion in an argument is frowned upon. When people get angry, sad, or scared in an argument or use emotional terms, this is seen as problematic. That's because emotion doesn't rely on facts and can distort logic. Even positive emotions make us less logical. In studies where participants were asked to solve logical problems after receiving either positive, negative, or neutral news, the participants who received neutral news performed the best. [1]

Does this mean that there's no place for emotion in arguments? No. In fact, emotion in arguments is unavoidable. When people express differing opinions, this almost always prompts a negative emotional reaction (such as anger, fear, or sadness). [2] So, instead of removing emotions completely from arguments, we need to learn how to work with and past them.

The first step to doing this is acknowledging your emotions and those of the other person. You can say something like "I know we're both feeling really upset right now," or "When X happened, I felt Y." It's important, here, to use accurate words for your feelings. If you use disproportionate words, like "That was heartbreaking," when it really made you feel sad or unheard, the other person might find your statement unbelievable or even hurtful.

Next, manage your emotions. This can be as simple as breathing more slowly and deeply. Taking deep breaths (diaphragmatic breathing) lowers your stress levels and helps you focus on what you're doing. [3] A good way to start with deep breaths is to follow the rule of fours. Just breathe in for a slow count of four, hold briefly, and breathe out for a slow count of four. Repeat this four times.

Finally, widen the gap between your thoughts and your response. When you respond right away in an argument, you're more likely to say something emotionally driven that you might later regret. Instead, pause for a count of three before replying to anything. Just a few seconds can keep you from saying something emotional that you regret.

"You Never Listen!"

What can you do if the person you're arguing with is the one using illogical arguments and following negative tendencies? Of course, stopping an argument in the middle to offer a helpful lesson on logical fallacies will probably not end well. Let's look at a few alternatives to keep an argument productive, even when the other person is being unreasonable.

First, figure out why they are being unreasonable. Some people act unreasonably in arguments because they don't really want to solve anything. They just want to fight. When people use insults and circular logic and aren't willing to back up their arguments or respond to questions, this is a good sign that they just want to fight. In that case, step away. If you're fighting with a loved one or colleague, you should plan when and how to continue the argument when you're both in a better place.

Sometimes, however, people act unreasonably simply because they have strong feelings about a topic or aren't skilled at structuring their statements logically. In this case, draw them out with questions to discover the root of their seemingly illogical statements. Perhaps the person you're fighting with claims that you never listen to them. Although this probably isn't true, it shows that they feel very strongly about the idea of not being heard. You can ask questions like, "Can you give some examples of times when I didn't listen?" or "What can I do to make you feel more heard?" You can also help to filter the conversation to make it more relevant, for instance by suggesting, "Did you feel unheard today at dinner?" Finally, you can help the other person feel understood by summarizing for understanding, i.e., "It sounds like I often look at my phone when we're talking, which makes you feel like I'm not listening. Is that true?"

Of course, drawing out the other person's thoughts beyond illogical statements or emotions doesn't mean you should stop arguing your own side. Once you understand their argument, for instance, that you are often on your phone during conversations, you can offer your own side. This could be, "Sometimes I'm on my phone when you start a conversation with me and I can't put it down right away to listen. If you can give me a minute to finish what I'm doing before we have the conversation, I think it will go better."

This is particularly important in arguments with people who won't listen to your side. Maybe, when you try to explain your position, the other person just keeps restating the same argument, for instance, "No, no, Y politician is better because they're fairer about taxes!" You give a hundred reasons why X politician is actually better, pointing out the problems with politician Y, but the other person stands firm without providing any more evidence. This kind of argument is extremely frustrating, but in most cases, it can be resolved using the same procedure mentioned above.

Very often, people aren't willing to listen because they feel they aren't being heard. This is especially the case if you're trained in logical thinking and the other person isn't. They might feel unable to make a stronger argument, but also feel that you are walking circles around them or trying to make them feel unintelligent.

So, make sure that the other person feels heard first by asking questions and acknowledging their point of view. You can say, for instance, "Okay, I agree that politician Y has some good ideas about inheritance taxes. Personally, I still disagree with what politician Y says about income and housing taxes, though." Once the other person feels like you are listening, they are much more likely to listen to you, too.

If you do everything, including asking questions, finding points of agreement, and summarizing for understanding, but the other person still won't listen, this probably isn't the right time or place for the argument. Maybe it isn't even a good topic for an argument. If possible, let the argument go and move on to something else. If it's essential that you and the other person have this argument and resolve it, then find other circumstances and try again.

Trying to understand the other person's argument doesn't mean that you're giving in to their opinion or that you think they're right. It just means that you want to understand their logical argument so that you can respond logically, too.

Cognitive Dissonance

One common issue in arguments is cognitive dissonance. Cognitive dissonance is an uncomfortable state when a person tries to hold two contradictory opinions. [4] For instance, let's say that you consider yourself to be a polite and attentive person, but one day are accused of looking at your phone all the time. You'll be thrown into a state of cognitive dissonance – are you polite or not? You also experience cognitive dissonance in an argument if the other person makes good, believable points that contradict your own.

Cognitive dissonance is an uncomfortable state, so most people will try to get out of it as quickly as possible. [5] The way to end cognitive dissonance is to either disregard the new information, disregard your old opinions, or find a way to believe both. In the phone example, you might decide that you are polite and you don't look at your phone at all. You might change your mind to believe that you actually have a problem with checking your phone. Or you might deduce that you are a polite person who sometimes gets distracted by your phone.

In the context of arguments, people often avoid cognitive dissonance by disregarding other opinions right away. This can make it very difficult to convince the person you're talking to that you are correct. It can also make the other person unwilling to listen to you at all.

So, instead, make room for the other person to find a way to believe both what you're saying and what they originally believed, when appropriate. You can do this in several ways. The first is by finding points of agreement, "We can both agree that taxes are important but can easily be done wrong." You can then offer a conditional compromise, "I think that politician Y's tax policy can work in some cases, but politician X's work better in others." Or you can find a way to bridge the person's old beliefs with your argument, "I know that you like politician Y because they have fairer taxes. But I think that politician X's taxes are actually fairer because he distributes the burden of taxation more equally."

With some help, you can make it much more likely that the other person will accept at least a part of your argument. At the same time, of course, you need to resolve your own cognitive dissonance productively, without completely disregarding either the other person's argument or your own.

Action Steps

Consider your own unhelpful tendencies in arguments. I, for instance, often go silent or walk away, which I'm working on not doing. At the same time, consider what the people around you tend to do in arguments. Do they yell or get sarcastic? Do they have the same tendencies as you do? If possible, sit down with the most important people in your life when you are both calm and work out some ground rules for arguments. Maybe you both promise to take deep breaths if you start raising your voices, or maybe you agree that you won't bring hyperbole into the argument.

If the people around you aren't excited to discuss ground rules, make rules for yourself. Even if you can't affect other people's behavior, you can make sure that you are arguing in the right way, which may influence those around you to do the same.

Finally, practice getting to the root of others' arguments with questions and logic. This doesn't have to be in a heated argument – you can simply practice asking questions about people's opinions and how they view the world. The more you practice this, the better you'll be at it when an argument does start.

With all this in mind, you can keep your arguments from spiraling out of control – at least most of the time. It might never be possible to have an argument without a few misunderstandings or negative tendencies, but you can significantly improve the quality of your arguments with practice.

What happens, though, when you argue with someone who seems completely misinformed? We all have a few people in our lives who believe something so different from what we think is true that it's almost impossible to have a conversation with them, let alone a good argument. How can you argue with such people? And more importantly, how can you tell if you're the misinformed one in an argument?

Chapter Summary

- In arguments, there are a few common unhelpful tendencies, including raising one's voice, becoming sarcastic or silent, and using hyperbole.
- Emotions can cloud logic, but there is still a place for emotion in arguments. Simply acknowledge the emotion and control it, for instance with deep breaths and pauses before speaking.
- Many people seem to have illogical or emotional beliefs. Sometimes, they just want to fight, in which case you should walk away. Often, though, they have an important argument that can be drawn out with good listening and questions.
- People experience cognitive dissonance when they need to reconcile two different and contradictory beliefs. This can lead to people disregarding new information or merging the two beliefs into a new opinion.

7

THE BAT AND THE BALL

M ost people, even the smartest, struggle to answer this simple arithmetic problem.

A bat and a ball together cost a dollar and ten cents. The bat costs a dollar more than the ball. How much does the ball cost?

Most people will answer quickly and confidently that the ball costs ten cents. This is as straightforward as it is wrong. In fact, the ball costs five cents, while the bat costs a dollar and five cents. Even more interestingly, the smarter you are, the more likely you are to answer questions like this incorrectly. [1] This is because intelligent people tend to rely on mental shortcuts and tricks, like the illusions we talked about in <u>Chapter Five</u>, and are more confident of their answers.

The same thing can happen in arguments. So often, we are sure that we are right, and that the other person's argument is wrong. And almost equally often, we find that the other person's point of view is also valid, which can be hard to accept. Let's have a look at what makes someone foolish or smart in an argument. Is the smart person the one who has all the facts and the best logic? Is the foolish person the one who believes something that sounds completely outlandish?

The truth, as always, is much more complicated. In an argument, the only foolish person is the one who refuses to listen to another point of view. Otherwise, anyone and everyone can have something valuable to contribute to an argument. This contribution can be new facts, an interesting view, or simply more knowledge about how the opposing side views things.

In some cases, this is easy to imagine. In an argument with a child, for instance, you probably won't learn facts or logic that you don't know, but you might gain a different perspective on a topic like homework or bedtime. If you argue with someone who has just started to learn about a topic in which you're an expert, again you might not learn new information, but you might get better at presenting the basics of your field in a widely understandable way. In other cases, it's a bit harder to see what you can learn from an argument.

Let's look at an argument that can be hard to accept: lifeboat ethics. Garret Hardin proposed the idea of lifeboat ethics as a way to decide whether or not to help people living in poverty. According to him, planet earth is like a lifeboat that's already filled to capacity. If we try to help everyone, eventually, there won't be enough resources for any of us. So, we should prioritize our own lives instead of helping people living in poverty. [2]

Of course, there's a strong argument against this. Many people argue that we should help others in poverty, even if it is difficult. There is plenty of research that backs this up and we can argue for hours, but if we refuse to look at Hardin's point at all, that's foolish. Instead, it's important to acknowledge the point of validity in his argument: We don't have enough resources for everyone to have the lifestyle of the richest among us. Instead, it's better to see the value in his argument, even if it's small. Maybe it's best to help people living in poverty, while preserving our resources by finding more sustainable solutions.

In most cases, even the most outlandish or foolish-sounding opinion has some good points to back it up – otherwise, no one would believe it. Of course, there are caveats: People sometimes argue an illogical position for various reasons, such as avoiding feeling dumb, purposefully playing devil's advocate, or simply wanting to fight. In that case, what you learn from the argument is more likely to be something about the person you're arguing with, such as that they enjoy debating or don't like to admit when they're wrong.

The OCEANs Within

In fact, some people struggle much more than others to admit when they are wrong. Whether or not one accepts defeat easily depends a lot on their personality type. Trait psychologists have determined the Big Five personality traits, which everyone has more or less. These are Openness, Conscientiousness, Extraversion, Agreeableness, and Neuroticism, easy to remember by the acronym OCEAN. [3] Together, these traits describe most aspects of our personalities, from how much we enjoy going to work every day to how quickly we get angry during arguments. You can imagine the traits like a sliding scale: every person has every trait, while some people are, for instance, more or less extroverted. Let's quickly go through the Big Five and how each of them affects the arguments we have.

Openness – your acceptance of new experiences, activities, and opinions. If you dislike routines and always want to learn something, you probably score higher on tests of Openness. People who are more open tend to be more accepting of opposing arguments. They also find it easier to combine their previous views with new information and update their mental models. [4] When you argue with an open person, you are more likely to find a resolution that balances your original opinions.

Of course, the opposite is also true – people who are less open struggle more to accept new information and differing opinions. When you are arguing with someone who isn't very open, make sure to provide lots of middle ground and positive links between your two differing opinions.

Conscientiousness – the trait of carefulness, diligence, and attention to detail. If you are punctual, detail-oriented, and don't like to move away from a task before it's finished, you probably also score high on tests of Conscientiousness. In arguments, conscientious people tend to focus on the facts and logic of an argument and want any statement to be thoroughly proven. [5] They may focus on small details or technicalities instead of the big picture and may struggle to reach a conclusion. When you are arguing with someone who is very conscientious, make sure to have a well-researched and logical argument and frequently summarize for understanding to keep things moving.

If, on the other hand, you are arguing with someone who isn't very conscientious, you may find that they get distracted and bring unrelated topics into the argument. When arguing with someone who isn't conscientious, be clear about the topic of the argument and gently keep the other person on track by circling back to that topic.

Extraversion – your desire to be around people and to be a leader. If you feel more energized when you are with other people and are talkative and assertive, you probably score higher on tests of extroversion. Very extroverted people tend to start and join arguments more frequently and with more enthusiasm. [6] They are usually masters of the rebuttal. Extroverted people may also be more interested in the conversation than the argument, so they might bring in a wider range of topics. [7] When arguing with an extroverted person, focus on your responses to the points they make and on emotion and conversation over pure logic.

Less extroverted people accordingly avoid arguments and tend to have slower, more thoughtful, and more problem-based arguments. [8] When arguing with someone who isn't extroverted, be sure to give them plenty of time to think about their responses without trying to push the argument forward quickly.

Agreeableness – the trait of empathy, helpfulness, and putting others' needs above your own. If you usually make decisions based on what will benefit other people, you probably score higher on tests of agreeableness. Agreeable people tend to avoid arguments and, when they do argue, tend to accept defeat quickly – even to the detriment of their own needs and opinions. [9] When arguing with an agreeable person, be sure to ask lots of questions and acknowledge the useful and interesting parts of their opinions.

Meanwhile, less agreeable people are more argumentative and are unlikely to change their opinions based on societal pressures. When arguing with someone who isn't agreeable, accept that the most likely outcome may be agreeing to disagree. At the same time, avoid emotional arguments – they probably won't work well.

Neuroticism – your disposition to experience negative emotions, such as anger, sadness, and self-consciousness. If you often take things personally and seem to experience a broader and deeper range of emotions than people around you, you probably also score higher on neuroticism tests. Neurotic people tend to be more emotional in arguments and take criticism personally. [10]

When arguing with a neurotic person, give them time and space to cool down and gather their thoughts. Also, be sure to use nonjudgmental language and plenty of "I" statements – "I was sad that we couldn't agree on our weekend plans."

Less neurotic people, however, tend to be calmer and more collected in arguments. When arguing with someone who isn't neurotic, leave space for their emotions – just because they aren't openly sad or upset doesn't mean they aren't feeling that way.

Of course, everyone has each of these traits to some degree. That means that you might be arguing with someone who is, for instance, very open but also very conscientious. This person might be interested in your opinion and ready to change their own beliefs – but only if you make a sound, logical, thorough argument.

No matter your personality or the personality of the person you're arguing with, one of the most difficult things is admitting when you're wrong. Sometimes, you start an argument with every confidence that you're right, only to find out that you aren't. Maybe you reach a compromise, or maybe you are faced with the prospect of admitting that you were simply wrong. Maybe you even find that you were being foolish about something. When this happens, how can you admit defeat gracefully and productively?

"I Was Wrong And I'm Sorry."

Why don't all arguments end with apologies and admission of wrongdoing from one or both sides? Unfortunately, it is very difficult for most people to admit when they have done something wrong. It goes against their sense of self. Worse, not apologizing can actually boost self-esteem. [11]

On top of that, admitting that you're wrong goes against feelings of superiority. Almost everyone feels superior to some extent; it's an important evolutionary adaptation. People need to believe that they are right, at least most of the time, to have high self-esteem and function well in the world. [12] Unfortunately, if unchecked, the sense of superiority can go too far and become a superiority complex. A superiority complex is simply the feeling that you are right – about everything, all the time, when arguing with anyone. Along with personal biases, this can make an admission of wrongdoing even more difficult. So, if you find yourself believing that you are right all the time in every situation, make sure to examine that closely. See how it might tie in with your biases and do your best to look for contradictory information that might make sense. No one can be right 100% of the time.

Because of all this, many people don't admit that they are wrong, even when they are. Why is it important to admit when you're wrong, then, even though it can be difficult? Not admitting when you're wrong isn't very socially graceful. Worse, it can actually hurt you. In the last chapter, we talked about cognitive dissonance, the uncomfortable feeling you get when trying to hold two separate, incompatible opinions. [13] If you don't resolve an argument through compromise or the mutual acceptance of one correct opinion and an apology, you also won't resolve your cognitive dissonance. This is why you might find yourself replaying parts of an argument in your head for days or continuing to feel guilty and worried even after the argument has ended. On the other hand, an apology and admission of wrongdoing show that you are compassionate, thoughtful, and logical.

The first step to admitting that you are wrong is acknowledging it yourself. If you say you are wrong and apologize just to end an argument, you aren't doing anyone any favors. In fact, you'll probably still feel cognitive dissonance and may have trouble getting past the argument. It can be difficult to admit that you are wrong, so take yourself through it slowly. Take as much time as you need to really believe it. Try looking at different opinions, perhaps online, or repeat to yourself the points that the other person made. Think deeply about not only what you were wrong about, but also why you were wrong. Perhaps you argued that coffee prevents cancer, which was wrong, but you felt very strongly about it because this belief helps you feel good about your morning cup of coffee.

Next, admit that you were wrong to the other person. In the case of an academic argument, this is usually enough. You might say, for instance, "I was wrong about coffee causing cancer. I see now that you're right – it actually doesn't have any effect." In a personal argument, though, you often need to go a step further by following this up with an apology and a plan of action. "I was wrong to contradict you in front of our friends. I'm sorry. It won't happen again."

Admitting that you were wrong when you are being foolish doesn't always feel good, but it's important. It resolves cognitive dissonance, shows that you care about the person you're arguing with, and can even bring your relationship with the other person closer. Most importantly, it keeps you from being the person who is acting irrationally or foolishly in an argument.

Respect – Even When It Isn't Easy

The final part of not being foolish in an argument, beyond being ready to learn from other points of view, understanding the other person, and acknowledging when you are wrong, is respecting the person you are arguing with. Of course, respect is vital for maintaining a positive relationship with anyone, but it also has a deeper psychological purpose. When you respect someone who disagrees with you, it de-escalates the conflict and makes it easier for you to accept the benefits of the opposing viewpoint. [14]

So, how can you be respectful, even when arguing with someone with a view that is completely against what you believe? The first step is to keep in mind that the other person's views are separate from the person. For instance, you might disagree with every one of your uncle's political beliefs, but still respect and enjoy being around your uncle. This can be difficult to remember if your first interaction with someone is an argument, but it is still equally true.

Next, find the underlying reason why the person believes what they do. As we discussed in the previous chapter, every argument has a root. Maybe your uncle loves football, which you dislike and never play or watch. It can be hard to respect the fact that he loves a sport that you dislike, but maybe he loves it because of all his good childhood memories of playing football and going to games with his father. Even if the belief is hard to understand, the root of the belief is usually something you can empathize with and respect.

Then, be respectful in your language. Never use personal attacks or rude names in any argument – all of your rebuttals should be directed at your uncle's argument, not your uncle himself. Meanwhile, try to use neutral words to describe complex topics, instead of terms that might be full of political baggage.

Finally, step away from arguments that you can't handle respectfully. If you sense an argument slipping into name-calling and losing respect, politely ask to continue the conversation later or not to discuss the topic at all. In almost every situation, it's more important to maintain mutual respect than to keep pushing when an argument isn't going anywhere. After all, you see your uncle at least a few times a year and want to have a positive relationship.

Action Steps

Moving forward, keep in mind your personality and the personality of those around you. Starting with yourself, think about where you fall on the sliding scale of personality traits and how this affects your arguments. Are you particularly extroverted, which can make you seek arguments out? Are you quite agreeable, which can mean that you end arguments with compromises that don't meet your own needs? No side of the scale is any better or worse than the others. Having different personality traits simply means that you'll need to keep various things in mind during your arguments to ensure they are positive and productive.

Once you've thought about your own personality, look at the personalities of those around you. Maybe you and your spouse have productive arguments because you are both open to new ideas. Or maybe you tend to clash with your coworker often because you are very conscientious, and they are less so. Then, plan how to have better, more respectful arguments with each of these people.

For reference, here are the Big Five personality traits once more:

- Openness – your acceptance of new experiences, activities, and opinions.

- Conscientiousness – the trait of carefulness, diligence, and attention to detail.
- Extroversion – your desire to be around people and to be a leader.
- Agreeableness – the trait of empathy, helpfulness, and putting others' needs above your own.
- Neuroticism – your disposition to experience negative emotions, such as anger, sadness, and self-consciousness.
- For a shortcut, you can remember these five personality traits with the helpful mnemonic OCEAN.

In the bat and the ball problem, people who get the wrong answer sometimes struggle to believe they are wrong. Instead of admitting defeat, they explain that they misread the problem or that it was confusing. The same thing happens in arguments, too – it can be tough to accept that you are wrong about something, especially if it's a strong opinion. Be conscious of this. Don't let the bat and the ball fool you.

Chapter Summary

- You can learn something from any argument – the only foolish thing to do is not to listen to opposing ideas.
- Everyone has different degrees of the Big Five personality traits, which affect how they argue.

For better arguments, understand the personality of the people you are arguing with.

- Not admitting when you're wrong can cause problems like cognitive dissonance and superiority complexes. Meanwhile, admitting when you are wrong can show respect for the other person and help you move on.
- Respect is essential in arguments – make sure you separate the argument from the person and understand the roots of why they believe what they do to maintain this respect. If needed, just step away from the argument.

IN THE FOOTSTEPS OF CHURCHILL AND CICERO

Churchill lived in the United Kingdom decades ago and argued passionately for his countrymen to join World War II. His choice of words and the tone in which he spoke them had a huge impact on the world.

Cicero lived centuries before Churchill, and before any of us, in Ancient Rome. His arguments against Caesar and against the problems of his day had a broad impact, even today, because of his focus on his gestures and presence.

Although these two men might seem very different at first glance, they are similar in one important way. Both men prioritized body language, tone, and expressions just as much as logic and facts. This continues to be as important today as it was hundreds of years ago. Even if you say all the right words with all the best logic, if you use the wrong tone or expression, you might fail to get your point across properly. In this chapter, we'll take a closer look at why body language matters so much – and how to use it to your advantage.

Wink, Shrug, Smile

Body language includes any movement or gesture that you make, your expression, tone, posture, and how you interact with others' personal space. In any conversation, body language does one of three things. It either reinforces your point, contradicts your words, or substitutes for speech entirely. [1]

Imagine that you are arguing with a coworker. You might say, "I really want to work this out," accompanied by a gesture: your hands outstretched in front of you, palms facing up. This is seen as a gesture of openness and acceptance in most societies. Your coworker will see the gesture, reinforcing your statement, and be more likely to believe you.

On the other hand, you might say, "I really want to work this out," along with a different gesture: arms folded across your chest, head tilted down. This gesture reads as angry and closed off, which contradicts your statement and might make your coworker less likely to believe that you are working towards a positive solution.

Gestures can also replace words completely. If you stomp up to your coworker's desk with a scowl, they will know right away that you are unhappy about something and that an argument is probably coming. Replacing words with gestures is actually very common – we nod or shake our heads, shrug our shoulders, or roll our eyes almost as often as we say something out loud.

Your body language may even be more important than your words. People are able to process body language more quickly than spoken language, so it tends to be the first thing to influence their reactions to you. [2] Just think of the last time you saw one of your friends and they smiled and waved – even before they said hello, you understood that they were excited to see you and felt more excited to see them. Or think of the last time you saw one of your friends with hunched shoulders and a frown – you knew right away that they weren't feeling their best. This is also why we tend to have gut feelings about people before we get to know them.

Interestingly, your body language affects not only the person you're talking to, but your own mental state as well. When you have a more assertive posture, such as standing with your shoulders back and your head up, you feel stronger and more confident than, for instance, sitting and hunching forward. [3] That's because people have two systems: the confident, friendly approach system and the nervous, uncomfortable inhibition system. [4] When the approach system is activated, you feel more confident. You are more likely to seek new experiences and stand up for yourself – and simply changing your body language can activate the approach system. You can experience this for yourself. Just try standing with your feet hip-width apart, your head up, and a confident smile for a minute or so. See if doing so changes your mood.

Mastering body language is essential to having better arguments – and to any conversation you have. How can you both use your body language to your advantage and better understand the body language of those around you? Let's start with the ways that your expressions can affect your arguments.

Expressions

Facial expressions are so vital to conversation that we've found a way to include them in our written communication, too, in the form of emojis. From the smiley face to the angry red face, emojis are something that almost everyone understands in the same way. Unfortunately, the real facial expressions that inspired those emojis aren't as straightforward.

Take smiling, for instance. People tend to smile multiple times in conversation to be polite and show interest, but these are rarely expressions of happiness. [5] A smile that better indicates happiness, instead of just being polite, called a Duchenne smile, can be spotted by not only turned up corners of the mouth but also crinkles on the sides of the eyes. [6]

For better or for worse, facial expressions in arguments tend to be easier to read. If the other person looks angry, they probably are. This is because, while people have social reasons to smile politely, they rarely have a social reason to look angry if they aren't feeling that way.

When it comes to your own facial expressions in arguments, focus on your eyes. One of the best ways to diffuse an argument is to offer friendly eye contact (not direct staring – that is territorial and suggests that you may be ready for a fight). [7] Eye contact makes people feel more connected and open, which can reduce tension and ease an argument.

Gestures

Beyond expressions, how you move and stand has a huge impact on how your words are understood. Gestures are so important that they can replace speech completely, either through nods and shakes of the head or complete sign languages.

In the wide world of gestures, let's start with what to watch out for. Crossed arms or legs usually signal that the person is closed off and feels protective. If you find yourself crossing your arms, try letting your arms rest by your sides or on your lap to offer a more open, welcoming posture. This will make the other person feel more comfortable talking to you and can improve your feelings as well. If the other person has crossed arms, try handing them a pen, some paper, or a cup of water. This will get them to release the closed-off posture and can make them more open to listening to your opinion. [8]

Another thing to watch out for is blading. This is when you or the person you're talking to assumes a defensive position: their dominant shoulder pointing towards you, their nondominant shoulder pointing away. This is a classic fighting position because it protects the heart and stomach and keeps the dominant hand in front for defense. It's common in arguments when one person is feeling attacked or upset. If you find yourself doing this, try to turn towards the other person to show openness. If someone else does it, take a step back – literally. Giving them more space can help them feel more comfortable.

At the same time, keep your eye out for cues of nervousness. This includes clasping fingers, rubbing the neck, and hunching shoulders. These are all self-comforting gestures and show that you or the other person are feeling nervous and insecure. If appropriate, this is a good time to try to comfort the other person, such as by reaching for their hand or using some gentle humor (though this should never include making fun of the other person).

Finally, look out for gestures that signal boredom. One of the main ones is fidgeting with small objects or clothing. While it often signals boredom, as people are looking for another sensory input, it can also mean that someone is feeling nervous or is running out of time to have the conversation. [9] You can often tell which based on the other gestures a person is doing, i.e., fidgeting and hunched shoulders generally mean nerves, while fidgeting and looking at the clock mean boredom. Other signs of boredom include yawning, sighing, and changing the subject.

You can also use gestures to help diffuse or resolve an argument. Tilting your head to the side, for instance, expresses vulnerability and shows that you are listening. Making eye contact lets the other person know that you are trying to connect with them. Presenting open palms shows that you are open and interested in finding a middle ground.

You can also use subtle mirroring to help advance your point. Mirroring means using similar body language to the person you're talking to. We do a lot of this automatically: if someone smiles, you smile, and if they turn to look at something, you do too. Close friends and romantic partners tend to mirror each other often without realizing it. When you mirror someone, you emphasize the connection between you. Doing so can diffuse an argument, get you higher sales numbers, or encourage faster promotions. [10] Just be sure that you mirror subtly. A little goes a long way. If the other person nods and you nod vigorously in response, it can look confusing or comical.

Touch And Personal Space

When you cross your arms or mirror someone, your actions will be understood the same way by almost anyone from your society. Touch and personal space, however, come across wildly differently to different people. Imagine having an argument with your significant other. As you are starting to resolve things, they step closer, offer a smile, and tap their shoulder against yours.

You'll probably feel comforted and reassured that the two of you are still close, regardless of the disagreement.

Now imagine that you are resolving an argument with your boss. As things are wrapping up, your boss steps closer, smiles, and nudges their shoulder against yours. In the best case, this is weird or intimidating. In the worst case, it's downright creepy. While, for instance, offering open palms is read more or less the same way with your spouse and your boss, touch and personal space are understandably read very differently.

It's better to err on the side of caution when it comes to touch and personal space. A safe distance to stand from another person is about eighteen inches, although this varies between countries and cultures. Standing closer can indicate familiarity, as you would with family and close friends. It can also be threatening, especially when there's a height difference or uneven power dynamic. Just think of how worrisome it can be to have your boss towering over you. Especially in an argument, when tensions run high, it's better not to be too close and risk coming off as intimidating.

Touch is the same; avoiding casual touch in arguments is best. While some touch can be comforting or helpful, like ending an argument between family members with a hug, touch can also be stifling or frustrating. If you're upset with someone, you probably don't want to hold their hand right then and might pull away if they try, which can be hurtful for both people.

Tone

The last element of body language is your tone. While this is spoken, not reflected in how you move or act, it's still an important element of nonverbal communication. If someone says, "That was really helpful," it sounds kind, right? Well, not if they say it in a sarcastic or mocking tone. Almost more than what you say, how you say it matters in an argument.

There are four elements of your tone of voice: pitch, pace, volume, and timbre. [11] Pitch is how high or low your voice can go. For instance, you use a higher pitch at the end of sentences to show that you are asking a question. Lower pitches tend to seem more authoritative and respectful, while higher pitches can make you sound unsure and even untrustworthy. Unfortunately, people tend to get higher pitched (or "shrill") when they are upset, which can have a negative effect on how their statements are perceived. Instead, try to keep a low, calm voice while arguing.

Next is pace. Pace is how quickly or slowly you speak. When you're arguing, you tend to pick up the pace, speaking faster and faster to get your points out as quickly as possible. Instead, try to slow down. This gives the person you're talking to more time to understand what you're saying and makes you sound calmer and more considerate. Don't get too slow, though: that can be seen as offensive and patronizing. A good rule of thumb is to talk at about half the speed you want to. In the heat of the moment, this will sound like a normal pace.

Volume is, of course, how loud or quiet you are as you speak. Having too high a volume (yelling) is almost guaranteed to make your argument more emotional and less logical. Quieter voices, on the other hand, sound calmer and are more likely to encourage the person you're speaking with to listen.

The last aspect is timbre. This is the emotional quality of your voice. Your timbre can be sarcastic, calm, friendly, angry, and so on. Much of the meaning that people take from statements comes from the timbre of your voice, so it's the most important aspect to get right. You can practice managing your voice and taking note of your tone by recording yourself and playing it back, then making insights into how you sound. Then you can try to modify your timbre to be more in line with the tone you're going for.

Stop And Go

One final thing that your body language can do is keep you calm. This is essential in arguments – the calmer you are, the more you'll be able to make good points and understand the other person's points. You can use a few simple physical tricks to calm your mind through body language.

The first is to take deep breaths. As discussed in <u>Chapter Six</u>, deep breathing lowers stress levels and makes you feel calmer and more in control. If you take deep breaths before responding, you not only calm yourself down, but you also give yourself a moment to consider what you want to say and how you want to say it.

Another trick is in your posture. As we discussed, a more assertive posture makes you feel powerful, too. Stand up straight with your shoulders back and your arms relaxed by your sides. Right away, you'll feel more confident and in control.

It also helps to be still. We fidget when we are nervous or bored, and fidgeting can then make you even more anxious or bored. Instead, try clasping your palms together or laying your hands flat on your legs. Both gestures are calming and better for your mental state than fidgeting.

If being still doesn't work, you can use movement to stay calm. Breaking into jumping jacks in the middle of a heated debate isn't encouraged, but asking for a break and going for a brisk walk can improve your mood and clear your mind. This can be a good trick for arguments in general: If you know you need to have a debate with a friend or family member, and they enjoy a bit of exercise too, open the conversation on a walk. With both of you moving, it can be easier to have a calm and productive discussion. Of course, this only works if the topic of the debate isn't too emotional – you don't want to end up discussing a personal topic in public.

Action Steps

It's time to put all this knowledge about gestures into practice. Standing in front of a mirror, try out some of the postures and gestures that we discussed in this chapter. How do you look with crossed arms, a polite smile, or a bladed posture? Do you appear friendly, angry, or open to new ideas? Make sure you also try some of the gestures that you tend to do in arguments. If you don't like the vibe that your body language is giving, try to change it. Can you be more open or relaxed? Experiment until you've found gestures that work for you. Then, try them out over the next few days and see what kind of responses you get.

Many years ago, Cicero and Churchill wowed audiences by bringing body language into their speeches and arguments. You can do the same by using tried and true body language strategies to emphasize your arguments. This final piece gives you all the information about arguing you need. In the next chapter, we'll test your new argumentative skills with practical exercises.

Chapter Summary

- Body language includes facial expressions, gestures, personal space, and tone. It is nearly as important as anything you actually say.
- Eye contact signals openness to communicate.

- Avoid crossing your arms, blading (turning away from the person you're talking to), and hunched, closed postures. Instead, try to show open palms, tilt your head, and angle your body towards the person you're speaking with.
- Aim for about 18 inches of space between you and the person you're talking with.
- Your tone has four elements: pitch, pace, volume, and timbre. This is how high or low your voice is, how quickly you talk, how loudly you speak, and the emotion in your voice.

TEST YOUR ARGUMENTATIVE SKILLS

A re you ready to argue better?

In this chapter, we'll put your argumentative skills to the test. Why is this important? Because the only way to get better at something is to practice. The more you practice and test your critical thinking skills, forming logical arguments, and knowing the rules of engagement for good arguments, the better your real arguments will be. When you're really arguing, you'll be less likely to miss logical fallacies and more likely to see the motivations and ideas underlying sketchy logic. All it takes is putting what you know about arguing into practice.

As we go through the examples, keep in mind the building blocks of a better argument, as we discussed in Chapter Four. These are:

- The right reasons (you and the other person are both arguing to resolve something or reach a shared understanding, not just to fight)
- The right topic (you both agree on the topic and understand why it's important)
- The right time (you have enough time to start and finish the argument without rushing)
- The right place (you are in a comfortable, safe, private location)
- The right goal (such as solving a problem, finding the truth, or reaching a compromise)

When you build your argument on these blocks, you're more likely to have a productive and positive argument than without them. Now, let's get into the examples. I'll start with a short scenario of an argument. Begin by reading it, then consider what went wrong and how both people could have handled the situation better. Whenever you can, draw parallels to your own life. Have you seen or been part of an argument like the one described? How could things have gone better?

The Worst Dinner

One day, Kate and Rudy are eating dinner at a nice restaurant. They have just sat down to eat when Kate suddenly blurts out, "I still think you shouldn't have invited your mother for the whole week."

Rudy snaps back, "Yeah, well, I put up with your horrible mother for a month."

"That was five years ago!" Kate replies. The dinner is ruined – they send jabs at each other for the rest of the evening.

What went wrong?

First of all, Kate and Rudy aren't having an argument. They're fighting. As we discussed in Chapter One, arguments are logic-based conversations that seek to find a shared understanding of something. With fights, on the other hand, differing opinions are shared, often loudly and insultingly. You can tell it's a fight, not an argument, because both are just stating opinions. Fights can be important. Sometimes, you and another person just need to air your grievances without trying to resolve them. However, it isn't really possible to fight better – fights are by nature not very constructive.

Second, even if Kate and Rudy had wanted to argue constructively, this wasn't the right place or time. It's better to consult a brief mental checklist before starting or joining an argument. A restaurant usually isn't the right place to have an argument, and in this case, it certainly wasn't.

So, what should Kate and Rudy have done differently?

The problem here didn't really start in the restaurant. Kate is referencing an earlier argument ("I *still* don't think...") that clearly wasn't resolved. This is why it's important to finish any arguments that you do start – otherwise, bad feelings linger between the two people and the argument might restart with little provocation.

Since we can't go back in time, though, Kate should have avoided bringing up the issue at the restaurant. If she felt strongly about it and struggled to enjoy her meal, she could have said something like, "I feel bad that we didn't finish our conversation about your mother. Can we talk about it when we get home?"

Rudy, meanwhile, shouldn't have jumped on the argument, either. A better response would have been something like, "I'm sorry you feel that way. I think we need to talk about this more, too. Can we discuss it at home?" In any case, the worst choice was to bring up something that happened five years ago – this shows that Rudy was more interested in fighting than resolving anything, just like Kate was.

Arguments shouldn't happen if one or both people aren't ready to discuss productively. If you or your partner isn't in a good place to find solutions and move forward, try scheduling the argument for another time.

We Need To Talk

Maddy has been having a problem with one of her employees, James, for a while now. James seems to work more slowly than anyone else and keeps turning in assignments that are full of mistakes. Finally, Maddy decides to talk to him about it. She walks to James' desk when the rest of his coworkers are away and stands beside it, one hand resting on the desk, looking down at him.

"We need to discuss your work," Maddy says. "Do you have a few minutes to talk about it?"

"Okay," James replies. He has his hands folded together, his shoulder slumped, and his head down. "What seems to be the problem?"

Maddy is annoyed – it isn't that there seems to be a problem, there *is* one. She turns away slightly so that one shoulder is facing away from James and the other towards him and crosses her arms. "Your work has been below the standard that I'd expect."

"I understand," James says, fidgeting with his pen and looking away. "I'm sorry. I'll try to do better next time."

"Great." Maddy leaves and James goes back to work.

What went wrong?

Although both Maddy and James said more or less the right things, their body language was saying something different. Maddy's body language was angry and intimidating, from the blading to the crossed arms to standing over James' desk, while James' posture was nervous and defensive, with fidgeting, hunched shoulders, and slumped posture. This shows that neither of them went into the argument with the right attitude. As we saw in <u>Chapter Eight</u>, body language is often a better cue for how people are thinking and feeling than their words are.

Furthermore, the argument wasn't constructive. Neither Maddy nor James asked any questions to try to understand the other person's perspective which, as we saw in <u>Chapter Six</u>, is essential, especially when one person is nervous or the power dynamic is uneven. Because of this, neither of them really understood what the other person was saying. How exactly did Maddy find James' work unsatisfactory? And were there reasons why James might be struggling with the work and might need help? Since no one asked and neither person clearly expressed their opinions, we don't know.

What should James and Maddy have done differently?

First, Maddy should have recognized the power differences between them and planned the conversation accordingly. She should acknowledge that some people avoid arguing with an authority figure and plan to draw out James' side while providing her own feedback. Preferably, Maddy should have planned to hold the meeting in a neutral environment where they were both sitting and when James had been warned in advance, so that he could plan what he wanted to say.

James, meanwhile, needed to ask questions and be more assertive. If he didn't feel prepared, one good option would be to ask if it was possible to have the meeting later in the day after some preparation. Although it might seem that James did the right thing by apologizing and not arguing, especially if he knows he did poor work, it wasn't a good way to resolve the argument. He might still not know what he did wrong or how to proceed. And he might feel cognitive dissonance if he apologized just to end the argument without really meaning it. It would have been better to ask questions and make sure that his opinion was heard.

In any argument, standing up for the points you want to make and trying to understand the other person's points is vital. Especially in arguments with an uneven power dynamic, be sure to look at the other person's body language and tone as well as their actual words.

The Alien Argument

Amira and Neil are walking out of a new sci-fi movie, both happy and pleased as they chat about their favorite parts.

"You know," Neil says during a lull, "there really are aliens out there."

Amira laughs. "No way, you're crazy. We've been looking for years and no one has been able to prove that there are aliens, so there's no way that there are any."

Neil is a bit offended by her dismissal. "Come on. Either you admit that there are aliens out there, or you think that humans are so special that we're at the center of the universe."

"Ugh, I don't think I can talk about this with you," Amira says. "I can't believe you think that there are really little green men out there."

They change the subject, but the rest of the afternoon is tense.

What went wrong?

First, this argument was completely based on logical fallacies, as discussed in <u>Chapter Three</u>. Amira uses an appeal to ignorance (saying that aliens must not exist because we haven't been able to prove that they do). Neil follows this up with a false dilemma (either Amira agrees that there are aliens or is self-centered and naïve). Amira then finishes off with a straw man fallacy (claiming that Neil believes in little green men, which isn't what he said). Neither Amira nor Neil had an argument based on logic or facts, which means neither one could present a compelling argument.

Second, neither was open to the other's opinions. Both rejected the possibility of learning something new because they were convinced they were right. As we saw in <u>Chapter Seven</u>, going into an argument without planning to learn anything is quite foolish.

What should Amira and Neil have done differently?

Primarily, both of them should examine the logic behind their arguments. However, someone else using a logical fallacy doesn't necessarily mean that there's no factual basis to their argument. If Amira had asked Neil why he believes that there are extraterrestrials, she might have eventually gotten to the root of his beliefs. For instance, Neil might believe that there are extraterrestrials because he's seen studies about how vast the universe is and about water on Mars. So, he believes that it's very likely that there are other planets with some kind of life.

If Neil asked Amira why she believes that there aren't extraterrestrials, he might have eventually learned that she knows how rare it is for planets to be habitable and thinks that the series of circumstances leading to life are improbable. Perhaps they could have eventually agreed that there might be unintelligent life, like fungi or algae, on other planets, even if they still disagreed about whether there's intelligent life.

In most arguments, it's more important to focus on understanding the other person's opinion and on learning something, instead of focusing on making good points or convincing the other person to change their mind. Of course, in this case, it's also important to make sure that the argument has some good logical basis.

Baby Steps

Lindsey's mom, Maria, has been helping out a lot since Lindsey's new baby was born a few months ago. One day, Lindsey comes home from work to find Maria showing the baby some children's television.

"Mom!" Lindsey says. "Remember, we talked about not starting screen time for at least eighteen months!"

"Hm," Maria says, then silently puts away the phone and walks to the kitchen. Lindsey follows her.

"Mom, are you listening? This is important."

Maria still doesn't say anything.

"Oh my gosh," Lindsey says. "You always do this. Whenever there's some important parenting decision, you always think you know best. 'Oh, I raised three children, I'm amazing.' Well, I'm done!"

Maria walks away, leaving Lindsey alone in the kitchen.

What went wrong?

Lindsey and Maria followed some of the negative tendencies that we discussed in Chapter Six. Maria, of course, falls silent and walks away, refusing to engage in the conversation. Without engaging, Maria's feelings won't be known and she appears unwilling to even discuss the topic. Lindsey is giving in to some negative tendencies too, specifically hyperbole and sarcasm. She also doesn't handle her mother's silence well. Clearly, Maria isn't able to engage in a productive conversation now, but Lindsey keeps pushing her.

Since Maria didn't speak, it's hard to know exactly why she wasn't willing to talk. Maybe she's not very extroverted and tends to avoid arguments. Maybe they've had this discussion before, and it hasn't been productive, so she doesn't want to repeat it. Or maybe she's just in a bad mood today. It could even be that she did want to join the conversation but needed more time to think of her responses. No matter her reasoning, it would have been better to say something than to stay silent – otherwise, Lindsey won't know what was going on.

What should Lindsey and Maria have done differently?

Lindsey should have been more careful when she realized that her mother wasn't speaking. She could have either given her mother more time or asked calmly to have the discussion later once they'd had some time to cool down. Since Maria is her mother, Lindsey would know whether she was often silent because of her personality or whether this was a unique situation. In any case, she shouldn't have followed Maria to the kitchen or gotten hyperbolic and sarcastic.

Maria, for her part, should have spoken up. That could have been as simple as saying, "I don't think this is the right time to talk about this. Can we discuss it after the baby goes to bed?" If Maria doesn't say anything, there's no way for the argument to reach a positive resolution – after all, it takes two. Staying silent is never the answer.

It can be tempting to let negative tendencies win out, especially when the other person seems to be clearly at fault or is behaving poorly. No matter what the other person does, though, it's important to keep a clear head and try to move the argument forward productively – or find a different time to have it.

All Together Now

While these exercises are fictional, they reflect how arguments can really go. It's all too easy for an argument to turn into a fight or give way to illogical statements. And it's all too common for an argument to spiral into unhelpful behaviors from both sides. However, there are three common mistakes across many arguments, and if you know about them, you can avoid them.

One – Thinking that it's the other side's job to resolve something. In many arguments, especially when one person allows negative tendencies to take over, it can seem like it's only that person's job to resolve things, for instance by apologizing. And it can be true that one person really is the one who was wronged and the other is entirely to blame – but that is very, very rare. In almost every situation, the argument went wrong because of mistakes on both sides, and both people need to work together to resolve things. In the case of Maria and Lindsey, for instance, Lindsey might be waiting for her mother to apologize since she was the one who gave the baby screen time when Lindsey had asked her not to.

Two – Not taking enough interest in the other side. Arguments also go off the rails when the people involved are more interested in winning and promoting their own opinion than listening to the other person. In fact, this was the case in every single example argument above. If you're focusing on your next comeback when the other person is talking, instead of asking questions and trying to understand their beliefs, the argument is doomed to failure. This played out in the arguments between Neil and Amira and Maddy and James – in both arguments, neither side was really interested in what the other was saying, even though it sounded like a "proper" argument.

Three – Ad hominem attacks. Ad hominem fallacies are arguments that go against a person rather than an argument. Using these fallacies in an argument is a classic way for things to go wrong. When you start criticizing the person you're arguing with for their beliefs or personality, it's very unlikely that you'll get anywhere. It's harder not to use ad hominem attacks when discussing a personal problem, like in the Maria and Lindsey example, but it's still possible. Just make sure to separate the person from the action, for instance by saying, "I was sad when you gave the baby screen time even though I asked you not to."

Action Steps

After doing the exercises in this chapter, create your own. Look back on a few arguments you've had and focus on what you did really well and what you perhaps could have done better. Be kind to yourself – everyone does a few things in arguments they aren't proud of. What you do well matters just as much, and the most important thing is being aware of how you can improve and trying your best to do so.

Ideally, figure out a few patterns of your biggest strengths and weaknesses when it comes to arguing. Once you do that, you'll know exactly what to work on going forward and exactly which sections you might need to look back on. Then, pick just one thing that you'd like to work on and focus on that. This could be asking more questions, not being sarcastic, or getting better at knowing which arguments to walk away from. Whatever your goal is, focus on it for your next few arguments until it becomes second nature. Then pick something else to work on. This way, slowly, your arguments will get better and better.

Chapter Summary

- Testing your argumentative skills helps you draft better arguments, think more logically, and see other points of view more clearly.
- The building blocks of a better argument are the right reasons, topic, time, place, and goals.
- Three main factors drive arguments off course: thinking it's the other person's job to resolve the argument, not listening enough to the other side, and using ad hominem attacks.

AFTERWORD

As a teenager, I thought I was great at arguing because of one specific instance. A friend and I were arguing about whether or not gymnastics is a real sport. I said that it was; after all, there are points given for different skills and taken away for certain mistakes. Gymnasts train for hours, I added, and are as fit as any athlete in another sport.

My friend argued that it wasn't – there are no goals, no timers, and no objective way to decide who is better. He struggled to make his point, though, and I kept on with a barrage of reasons why I was right. In retrospect, he was trying to make the point that gymnastics isn't an *objectively judged* sport, but at the time, I wasn't interested in understanding that. I just wanted to win.

And I did win. Finally, my friend threw up his hands and said, "You're just too good at arguing. I don't want to talk about it anymore." I was very happy about this and I thought I was good at arguing because of that result. It was only much later that I realized that I wasn't. I was good at facts and logic but arguing is about a lot more than that. Later, I tried to stop arguing completely, which is an equally bad option. I hope that, through the course of this book, you saw that too.

Having better arguments means focusing not just on excellent logic and reliable facts but also on the other person's opinions and how you can learn, consider, and improve your relationship while arguing. This may seem too lofty a goal for a simple argument, but it is possible. By focusing on one step at a time, your arguments can get better and better until they are consistently positive experiences for both people.

This book provided a roadmap for how to do that. In Chapter One, we started the journey. We looked at what an argument is, from the definition of an argument itself to how arguments usually start and why we have them.

Chapter Two took things a step back – way back. We looked at how arguments evolved throughout history, from the parallel evolution of arguments in ancient societies to important figures in the history of arguments. We also looked at what the best arguers throughout time have in common.

In Chapter Three, we looked at how even reliable facts can go wrong through logical fallacies and how to overcome them with logical thinking. Chapter Three ended with a list of do's and don'ts for better arguing – a key to understanding the complexities of the time and place for your arguments.

Just like some people stop to ask for directions right away, while others only do in the direst situations, some people enjoy arguing while others always avoid it. Chapter Four examined why people feel so differently about arguing, for both helpful and unhelpful reasons. Chapter Four concluded with a checklist of the requirements for a productive argument and questioned whether arguments need to be won to be worthwhile (they don't).

Chapter Five got more personal with a look at the mistakes our brains can make when processing new information. Our instincts and biases lead us to argue when new information doesn't fit into what we know or believe, but it's possible to overcome this by taking an alternate route.

Chapter Six looked at the other half of the argument – the person you're arguing with. We discussed negative tendencies in arguments, such as raising voices or getting silent. Then we discussed how to handle these tendencies, which often come from valid emotional reasons, and how to look past others' illogical or emotional arguments to find the root of their beliefs.

Some people lash out when they get lost and take their annoyance out on others. In Chapter Seven, we looked at foolishness and respect in arguments. We discussed how different personalities can cause people to argue differently and how to deal with this. We also talked about the importance of looking at and respecting other points of view.

Chapter Eight was all about body language. We discussed the different kinds of body language that come up in arguments. We also explored how to better understand others' body language and use your own to your advantage, both for more effective communication and for remaining calm.

Finally, Chapter Nine puts your argumentative skills to the test with different examples. Testing your argumentative skills is the best and fastest way to improve your arguments – the more you practice, the better you'll get. With your map in hand, Chapter Nine gave a few possible routes and let you determine when they got off course.

Now, you have your roadmap spread before you, along with a better understanding of what it really means to improve your arguments. It's time to put it all into practice. You're ready to argue.

CONTINUING YOUR JOURNEY

 Those Who Keep Learning, Will Keep Rising In Life.

— CHARLIE MUNGER (BILLIONAIRE, INVESTOR, AND WARREN BUFFET'S BUSINESS PARTNER)

The most successful people in life are those who enjoy learning and asking questions, understanding themselves and the world around them.

In our Thinknetic newsletter we'll share with you our best thinking improvement tips and tricks to help you become even more successful in life.

It's 100% free and you can unsubscribe at any time.

Besides, you'll hear first about our new releases and get the chance to receive them for free or highly discounted.

As a bonus, you'll get our bestselling book *Critical Thinking In A Nutshell* & 2 thinking improvement sheets completely for free.

Go to thinknetic.net to sign up for free!

(Or simply scan the code with your camera)

SCAN ME

THE TEAM BEHIND THINKNETIC

Michael Meisner, Founder and CEO

When Michael got into publishing books on Amazon, he found that his favorite topic - the thinking process and its results, is tackled in a much too complex and unengaging way. Thus, he set himself up to make his ideal a reality: books that are informative, entertaining, and can help people achieve success by thinking things through.

This ideal became his passion and profession. He built a team of like-minded people and is in charge of the strategic part and brand orientation, as he continues to improve and extend his business.

Claire M. Umali, Publishing Manager

Crafting books is collaborative work, and keeping everyone on the same page is an essential task. Claire oversees all the stages of this collaboration, from researching to outlining and from writing to editing. In her free time, she writes reviews online and likes to bother her cats.

Davan O'Donnell, Writer

Davan is a writer with experience in psychology, international relations, and teaching. She loves making abstract or complex topics relatable and interesting. Davan has written a variety of pieces, from non-fiction and fiction books to articles and theses. Originally from the United States, she is now based in Prague.

Alfonso E. Padilla, Content Editor

Mexican editor with a background in journalism. Alfonso takes pride in his curiosity and cares deeply about learning. True to his formation, he prioritizes solid research and sources when reviewing texts. His main tool for editing is the use of questions.

Sandra Agarrat, Language Editor

Sandra Wall Agarrat is an experienced freelance academic editor/proofreader, writer, and researcher. Sandra holds graduate degrees in Public Policy and International Relations. Her portfolio of projects includes books, dissertations, theses, scholarly articles, and grant proposals.

Sheena Marie Orosco Peñaflor, Researcher

Sheena Marie Orosco Peñaflor has over 10 years of skills and expertise in e-commerce business management, web development, graphic design, and digital marketing. She also holds a degree in BS Nursing and has taught at the university level.

Ralph Escarda, Layout Designer

Ralph's love for books prevails in his artistic preoccupations. He is an avid reader of non-fictional books and an advocate of self-improvement through education. He dedicates his spare time to doing portraits and sports.

Josie Laica Oronos, Layout Designer

Josie Laica Oronos is a licensed teacher and teaches English to foreign language learners. Josie also loves to spend time with her dogs and cat.

REFERENCES

1. Back To The Basics

1. Evagorou, M., & Osborne, J. (2013). Exploring young students' collaborative argumentation within a socioscientific issue. *Journal of Research in Science Teaching, 50*(2), 209–237. https://doi.org/10.1002/tea.21076
2. Lin, S. S., & Mintzes, J. J. (2010). Learning argumentation skills through instrument in socioscientific issues: The effect of ability level. *International Journal of Science and Mathematics Education, 8*(6), 993–1017. http://dx.doi.org/10.1007/s10763-010-9215-6
3. Schwarz, B., & Asterhan, C. (2010). Argumentation and reasoning. In K. Littleton, C. Wood, & J. Kleine Staarman (Eds.), *International handbook of psychology in education* (pp. 137-176). Emerald Group Publishing.
4. Schwarz, B., & Asterhan, C. (2010). Argumentation and reasoning. In K. Littleton, C. Wood, & J. Kleine Staarman (Eds.), *International handbook of psychology in education* (pp. 137-176). Emerald Group Publishing.
5. Schwarz, B., & Asterhan, C. (2010). Argumentation and reasoning. In K. Littleton, C. Wood, & J. Kleine Staarman (Eds.), *International handbook of psychology in education* (pp. 137-176). Emerald Group Publishing.
6. Toulmin, S. (2003). *The uses of argument* (2nd ed.). Cambridge: Cambridge University Press. https://doi.org/10.1017/CBO9780511840005
7. Coyle, D. (2014, August 19). 10 surprising truths from the world's most successful talent hotbed. *Daniel Coyle*. https://danielcoyle.com/2014/08/19/10-surprising-truths-from-the-worlds-most-successful-talent-hotbed/
8. Mills, A. (2022). *How arguments work — A guide to writing and analyzing texts in college.* City College of San Francisco. https://human.libretexts.org/Bookshelves/Composition/Advanced_Composition/Book%3A_How_Arguments_Work_-_A_Guide_to_Writing_and_Analyzing_Texts_in_College_(Mills)

9. Purdue Owl. (n.d.). Classical arguments. Retrieved January 5, 2023, from https://owl.purdue.edu/owl/general_writing/academic_writing/historical_perspectives_on_argumentation/classical_argument.html

10. Brent, D. (1991). Young, Becker and Pike's "Rogerian" rhetoric: A twenty-year reassessment. *College English, 53*(4), 452–466. https://doi.org/10.2307/378020

11. Brent, D. (1991). Young, Becker and Pike's "Rogerian" rhetoric: A twenty-year reassessment. *College English, 53*(4), 452–466. https://doi.org/10.2307/378020

12. Mills, A. (2022). *How arguments work – A guide to writing and analyzing texts in college.* City College of San Francisco. https://human.libretexts.org/Bookshelves/Composition/Advanced_Composition/Book%3A_How_Arguments_Work_-_A_Guide_to_Writing_and_Analyzing_Texts_in_College_(Mills)

13. Mills, A. (2022). *How arguments work – A guide to writing and analyzing texts in college.* City College of San Francisco. https://human.libretexts.org/Bookshelves/Composition/Advanced_Composition/Book%3A_How_Arguments_Work_-_A_Guide_to_Writing_and_Analyzing_Texts_in_College_(Mills)

2. Why Ancient Arguments Matter To You

1. Seitz, F. Argumentation evolved: But how? Coevolution of coordinated group behavior and reasoning. *Argumentation 34*, 237–260 (2020). https://doi.org/10.1007/s10503-020-09510-6

2. Hansen, M. H. (1999). *The Athenian democracy in the age of Demosthenes: Structure, principles, and ideology* (J.A. Crook, Trans.), Oxford: Blackwell. (Original work published 1991)

3. Hansen, M. H. (1999). *The Athenian democracy in the age of Demosthenes: Structure, principles, and ideology* (J.A. Crook, Trans.), Oxford: Blackwell. (Original work published 1991)

4. Matilal, B. K. (1998). *The character of logic in India.* Albany, NY: State University of New York Press.

5. Matilal, B. K. (1998). *The character of logic in India.* Albany, NY: State University of New York Press.

6. Matilal, B. K. (1998). *The character of logic in India.* Albany, NY: State University of New York Press.

7. Hansen, C. (1983). *Language and logic in Ancient China.* Ann Arbor, MI: University of Michigan Press.

8. Duncombe, M., & Novaes, C. D. (2015). Dialectic and logic in Aristotle and his tradition. *History and Philosophy of Logic, 37*(1), 1–8. http://dx.doi.org/10.1080/01445340.2015.1086624
9. Tzu, S. (1963). *The art of war.* (S. Griffith, Trans.). Oxford University Press.
10. Butler. S. (2002) *The hand of Cicero.* London: Routledge.
11. Bray, R. (1995). "The power to hurt": Lincoln's early use of satire and invective. *Journal of the Abraham Lincoln Association, 16*(1), 39-58. http://hdl.handle.net/2027/spo.2629860.0016.106
12. Times of India Team. (2019, September 27). *Remembering Gandhi: Top 10 quotes by the Mahatma.* https://timesofindia.indiatimes.com/blogs/the-photo-blog/remembering-gandhi-top-10-quotes-by-the-mahatma/

3. The Case Of The Tech-Savvy Spinach

1. Ferrer, M. (2022, September 14). Scientists have taught spinach to send emails and it could warn us about climate change. *Euronews.* https://www.euronews.com/green/2021/02/01/scientists-have-taught-spinach-to-send-emails-and-it-could-warn-us-about-climate-change
2. Wong, M., Giraldo, J., Kwak, SY. et al. Nitroaromatic detection and infrared communication from wild-type plants using plant nanobionics. *Nature Mater 16,* 264–272 (2017). https://doi.org/10.1038/nmat4771
3. Wong, M., Giraldo, J., Kwak, SY. et al. Nitroaromatic detection and infrared communication from wild-type plants using plant nanobionics. *Nature Mater 16,* 264–272 (2017). https://doi.org/10.1038/nmat4771
4. Schwarz, B., & Asterhan, C. (2010). Argumentation and reasoning. In K. Littleton, C. Wood, & J. Kleine Staarman (Eds.), *International handbook of psychology in education* (pp. 137-176). Emerald Group Publishing.
5. Schwarz, B., & Asterhan, C. (2010). Argumentation and reasoning. In K. Littleton, C. Wood, & J. Kleine Staarman (Eds.), *International handbook of psychology in education* (pp. 137-176). Emerald Group Publishing.
6. Schwarz, B., & Asterhan, C. (2010). Argumentation and reasoning. In K. Littleton, C. Wood, & J. Kleine Staarman (Eds.), *International handbook of psychology in education* (pp. 137-176). Emerald Group Publishing.

7. Wilson, D. (2020). *A guide to good reasoning: Cultivating intellectual values.* University of Minnesota Libraries Publishing.
8. Carpenter, C. B., & Doig, J. C. (2006). Assessing critical thinking across the curriculum. Assessing Students' Learning. *New Directions for Teaching and Learning 1988*(34), 33-46. https://doi.org/10.1002/tl.37219883405
9. Mayo Clinic Staff. (n.d.). *Cancer prevention: 7 tips to reduce your risk.* Retrieved January 5, 2023, from https://www.mayoclinic.org/healthy-lifestyle/adult-health/in-depth/cancer-prevention/art-20044816
10. Cancer Treatment Centers of America. (2019, January 2). *Busting myths: Can coffee cause, cure or prevent cancer?* https://www.cancercenter.com/community/blog/2019/01/busting-myths-can-coffee-cause-cure-or-prevent-cancer
11. Brooks, A. W., & John, L. K. (2018). The surprising power of questions. *Harvard Business Review 96*(3), 60–67.
12. Brooks, A. W., & John, L. K. (2018). The surprising power of questions. *Harvard Business Review 96*(3), 60–67.
13. Brooks, A. W., & John, L. K. (2018). The surprising power of questions. *Harvard Business Review 96*(3), 60–67.
14. Schwarz, N., & Strack, F. (1991). Context effects in attitude surveys: Applying cognitive theory to social research. *European Review of Social Psychology* 2(1), 31-50. https://doi.org/10.1080/14792779143000015
15. Brooks, A. W., & John, L. K. (2018). The surprising power of questions. *Harvard Business Review 96*(3), 60–67.

4. Stuck In The Middle With You

1. Talisse, R., & Aikin, S. (2013). *Why we argue (and how we should): A guide to political disagreement* (1st ed.). Routledge. https://doi.org/10.4324/9780203797891
2. Talisse, R., & Aikin, S. (2013). *Why we argue (and how we should): A guide to political disagreement* (1st ed.). Routledge. https://doi.org/10.4324/9780203797891
3. Mercier, H. & Sperber, D. (2011). Why do humans reason? Arguments for an argumentative theory. *Behavioral and Brain Sciences, 34*(2), 57-74. https://ssrn.com/abstract=1698090
4. Mercier, H. & Sperber, D. (2011). Why do humans reason? Arguments for an argumentative theory. *Behavioral and Brain Sciences, 34*(2), 57-74. https://ssrn.com/abstract=1698090

5. Gordon, A. M., & Chen, S. (2014). The role of sleep in interpersonal conflict: Do sleepless nights mean worse fights? *Social Psychological and Personality Science, 5*(2), 168–175. https://doi.org/10.1177/1948550613488952

6. Mercier, H. & Sperber, D. (2011). Why do humans reason? Arguments for an argumentative theory. *Behavioral and Brain Sciences, 34*(2), 57-74. https://ssrn.com/abstract=1698090

7. Almost, Joan. (2013). Review: Conflict on the treatment floor: An investigation of interpersonal conflict experienced by nurses. *Journal of Research in Nursing, 19*(1), 38-39. https://doi.org/10.1177/1744987113485841

8. Yarnell, Lisa M., & Neff, K. D. (2013). *Self-compassion, interpersonal conflict resolutions, and well-being, self and identity, 12*(2), 146-159, https://doi.org/10.1080/15298868.2011.649545

9. Trepanier, S. (2022). How to engage in productive disagreements at work. *Continuing Education in Nursing, 53*(8), 344-345. https://doi.org/10.3928/00220124-20220706-03

5. Believe It Or Not

1. Fibonacci. (2017). *Zollner illusion* [Image]. Wikimedia Commons. https://commons.wikimedia.org/wiki/File:Zollner_illusion.svg

2. Ericsson, A., & Pool, R. (2016). *Peak: Secrets from the new science of expertise.* Houghton Mifflin Harcourt.

3. Ericsson, A., & Pool, R. (2016). *Peak: Secrets from the new science of expertise.* Houghton Mifflin Harcourt.

4. Bargh, J. A., & Morsella, E. (2008). The unconscious mind. *Perspectives on Psychological Science, 3*(1), 73-79. https://doi.org/10.1111/j.1745-6916.2008.00064.x

5. Bargh, J. A., & Morsella, E. (2008). The unconscious mind. *Perspectives on Psychological Science, 3*(1), 73-79. https://doi.org/10.1111/j.1745-6916.2008.00064.x

6. Rosling, H., Rosling, O., & Rönnlund, A. R. (2018). *Factfulness: Ten reasons we're wrong about the world - and why things are better than you think.* Sceptre.

7. Kahneman, D. (2011). Thinking, fast and slow. Farrar, Straus and Giroux.

6. The Other Half Of The Argument

1. Jung, N., Wranke, C., Hamburger, K., & Knauff, M. (2014). How emotions affect logical reasoning: evidence from experiments with mood-manipulated participants, spider phobics, and people with exam anxiety. *Frontiers in Psychology, 5*, 570. https://doi.org/10.3389%2Ffpsyg.2014.00570
2. Benlamine, M. S., Chaouachi, M., Villata, S., Cabrio, E., Frasson, C., & Gandon, F. L. (2015). Emotions in argumentation: An empirical analysis. *Proceedings of the Twenty-Fourth International Joint Conference on Artificial Intelligence.*
3. Ma, X., Yue, Z. Q., Gong, Z. Q., Zhang, H., Duan, N. Y., Shi, Y. T., Wei, G. X., & Li, Y. F. (2017). The effect of diaphragmatic breathing on attention, negative affect and stress in healthy adults. *Frontiers in Psychology, 8*, 874. https://doi.org/10.3389/fpsyg.2017.00874
4. Cooper, J. (2019). Cognitive dissonance: Where we've been and where we're going. *International Review of Social Psychology, 32*(1), 7. http://doi.org/10.5334/irsp.277
5. Cooper, J. (2019). Cognitive dissonance: Where we've been and where we're going. *International Review of Social Psychology, 32*(1), 7. http://doi.org/10.5334/irsp.277

7. The Bat And The Ball

1. West, R. F., Meserve, R. J., & Stanovich, K. E. (2012). Cognitive sophistication does not attenuate the bias blind spot. *Journal of Personality and Social Psychology, 103*(3), 506–519. https://doi.org/10.1037/a0028857
2. Hardin, G. (1974). *Lifeboat ethics: The case against helping the poor.* Psychology Today, 8, 38–43.
3. Matthews, G., Deary, I. J., & Whiteman, M. C. (2003). Personality traits. Cambridge, UK: Cambridge University Press.
4. Gronostay, D. (2019). To argue or not to argue? The role of personality traits, argumentativeness, epistemological beliefs and assigned positions for students' participation in controversial political classroom discussions. *Unterrichtswiss, 47*, 117–135. https://doi.org/10.1007/s42010-018-00033-4
5. Gronostay, D. (2019). To argue or not to argue? The role of personality traits, argumentativeness, epistemological beliefs and assigned positions for students' participation in controversial

political classroom discussions. *Unterrichtswiss, 47*, 117–135. https://doi.org/10.1007/s42010-018-00033-4

6. Gronostay, D. (2019). To argue or not to argue? The role of personality traits, argumentativeness, epistemological beliefs and assigned positions for students' participation in controversial political classroom discussions. *Unterrichtswiss, 47*, 117–135. https://doi.org/10.1007/s42010-018-00033-4

7. Thorne, A. (1987). The press of personality: A study of conversations between introverts and extraverts. *Journal of Personality and Social Psychology, 53*(4), 718-726. https://doi.org/10.1037/0022-3514.53.4.718

8. Thorne, A. (1987). The press of personality: A study of conversations between introverts and extraverts. *Journal of Personality and Social Psychology, 53*(4), 718-726. https://doi.org/10.1037/0022-3514.53.4.718

9. Gronostay, D. (2019). To argue or not to argue? The role of personality traits, argumentativeness, epistemological beliefs and assigned positions for students' participation in controversial political classroom discussions. *Unterrichtswiss, 47*, 117–135. https://doi.org/10.1007/s42010-018-00033-4

10. Larsen, R. J., & Ketelaar, T. (1991). Personality and susceptibility to positive and negative emotional states. *Journal of Personality and Social Psychology, 61*(1), 132–140. https://doi.org/10.1037//0022-3514.61.1.132

11. Okimoto, T. G., Wenzel, M., & Hedrick, K. (2013). Refusing to apologize can have psychological benefits (and we issue no mea culpa for this research finding). *European Journal of Social Psychology, 43*(1), 22-31. https://doi.org/10.1002/ejsp.1901

12. Ayim-Aboagye, D. (2018). Fundamental theorem of the theory of superiority complex. *International Journal of Emerging Trends in Science and Technology*. http://dx.doi.org/10.18535/ijetst/v5i7.05

13. Cooper, J. (2019). Cognitive dissonance: Where we've been and where we're going. *International Review of Social Psychology, 32*(1), 7. http://doi.org/10.5334/irsp.277

14. Eschert, S., & Simon, B. (2019). Respect and political disagreement: Can intergroup respect reduce the biased evaluation of outgroup arguments? *PLoS ONE, 14*(3), Article e0211556. https://doi.org/10.1371/journal.pone.0211556

8. In The Footsteps Of Churchill And Cicero

1. Oneri Uzun, G. (2020). A review of communication, body language and communication conflict. *International Journal of Psychosocial Rehabilitation, 24*(9), 2833-2844.
2. Ladewig, S., & Müller, C., Cienki, A., Fricke, E., Mcneill, D., & Teßendorf, S. (Eds.). (2013). *Body-Language-Communication: An international handbook on multimodality in human interaction.* (Handbooks of Linguistics and Communication Science Vol. 38, No. 1). De Gruyter Mouton.
3. Cuddy, A. (2019). *Presence: Bringing your boldest self to your biggest challenges.* Little, Brown, & Company.
4. Cuddy, A. (2016). *Presence: Bringing your boldest self to your biggest challenges.* Little, Brown, & Company.
5. Pease, A. (2017). *The definitive book of body language: How to read others' attitudes by their gestures.* London: Orion.
6. Schmidt, K. & Cohn, J. (2001). Human facial expressions as adaptations: Evolutionary questions in facial expression research. *Yearbook of Physical Anthropology.* http://dx.doi.org/10.1002/ajpa.20001.abs
7. Pease, A. (2017). *The definitive book of body language: How to read others' attitudes by their gestures.* London: Orion.
8. Cuddy, A. (2016). *Presence: Bringing your boldest self to your biggest challenges.* Little, Brown, & Company.
9. Morris, D. (2012). *Peoplewatching: The Desmond Morris guide to body language.* London: Vintage Digital.
10. [10] Morris, D. (2012). *Peoplewatching: The Desmond Morris guide to body language.* London: Vintage Digital.
11. Patel, A. D. (2012). Sound elements: Pitch and timbre. *Oxford Academic.* https://doi.org/10.1093/acprof:oso/9780195123753.003.0002

DISCLAIMER

The information contained in this book and its components is meant to serve as a comprehensive collection of strategies that the author of this book has done research about. Summaries, strategies, tips and tricks are only recommendations by the author, and reading this book will not guarantee that one's results will exactly mirror the author's results.

The author of this book has made all reasonable efforts to provide current and accurate information for the readers of this book. The author and their associates will not be held liable for any unintentional errors or omissions that may be found.

The material in the book may include information by third parties. Third-party materials are comprised of opinions expressed by their owners. As such, the author of this book does not assume responsibility or liability for any third party material or opinions.

Printed in Great Britain
by Amazon

34363775R00091